THE BEGINNING DRESSAGE BOOK

Kathryn Denby-Wrightson

and Joan Fry

PRENTICE
HALL PRESS
EQUESTRIAN
B O O K S

New York   London   Toronto   Sydney   Tokyo   Singapore

To those who taught us:

George, Wesley, and Juvialle
John and Sassafras

This book is lovingly dedicated

Prentice Hall Press
15 Columbus Circle
New York, New York 10023

Published in 1987 by Prentice Hall Press
A Division of Simon & Schuster, Inc.
Originally published by Arco Publishing, Inc.

Library of Congress Cataloging-in-Publication Data

Denby-Wrightson, Kathryn.
  The beginning dressage book.
  Includes Index.
  1. Dressage. I. Fry, Joan, joint author.
II. Title.
SF309.5.D46   798.2′4   80-16950
ISBN 0-668-04969-3

Manufactured in the United States of America

10 9 8 7 6 5

Contents

Acknowledgments

The authors would like to thank the following people for their help and encouragement:

Judy Bowen
David J. Bradley, author of *Expert Skiing*
Hillair Evans-Bell
John Fry
John Havey
Pat Joy
Pam Knights
Mike and Saleta Mosley, Mary's Tack and Feed
Emil Rueb, The Camera Shop of Hanover, Inc.
Anne Steinbach
William Steinkraus
George Wrightson, DVM

Special thanks to Bachelor, Pam Knights' Thoroughbred-Quarter Horse gelding. Without our friends and our horses, this book would not have been written.

Preface

Are you a horse owner who wishes your horse would cooperate with you just a little more willingly?

Then *The Beginning Dressage Book* is for you.

This is like no other book about horsemanship you'll ever read—a practical, down-to-earth handbook that explains how to develop your own skills as a rider and how to re-educate your horse into a smooth, relaxed, *responsive* horse that's a joy to ride.

Co-authored by a professional trainer, *The Beginning Dressage Book* also:

1. Tells you how to buy the right bit and saddle for your horse.
2. Explains how to correct your horse's bad habits on the lunge line.
3. Gives you an insider's tips on what judges look for in a dressage test.

We believe that beginning dressage can help any horse become more capable at what he does—no matter what it is—and more enjoyable to ride. *The Beginning Dressage Book* tells you how to train *your* horse in beginning dressage in your own backyard, without a lot of expensive and unnecessary equipment.

It asks the questions every beginner in dressage wants to know and answers them in concise, easy-to-follow language.

1

It helps you recognize the goals you're working toward in every stage of training—on the lunge line, in the riding ring, even out on the trail—and what to do to achieve them, step by careful step.

It deals with the problems that most riders, and most horses, encounter when they're learning.

We advise you to sit down and read *The Beginning Dressage Book* straight through, from cover to cover, before you start working. We do this for two reasons: so we can avoid repeating information, and so you can see for yourself the logical sequence of steps involved in training. There is certain basic information that anyone training a horse in dressage has to know, and you *have* to learn the basic steps before you go on to the more advanced ones. Once you've read the book through and begin working, you'll probably find that you don't need some of the information—your horse may never canter disunited, for instance. But if you do run into a problem, you'll find out why you're having it and what to do about it.

The "I" in *The Beginning Dressage Book* is the voice of Kathryn Denby-Wrightson, a Canadian-born trainer, teacher, and judge who has been competing successfully since she was 12 years old. Since receiving her British Horse Society Instructor certificate from Colonel Ian Dudgeon of the Irish Olympic team, Ms. Denby-Wrightson has studied dressage under some of the most prestigious instructors in the world: Colonel Alois Podhajsky, former director of the Spanish Riding School in Vienna; Major Hans Wilkne, coach of the Swedish Olympic team; Gunnar Anderson, coach of the Danish Olympic team; E. Schmidt-Jensen, Hans Meuller, and F. Rochowansky, among others. She has trained many different horses and competed at every level of dressage, from Training Level to Grand Prix.

Her co-author, Joan Fry, is a writer and backyard horse owner who has written numerous articles about horses and horse people but who didn't know impulsion from Adam until she began taking dressage instruction from Ms. Denby-Wrightson. *The Beginning Dressage Book* first saw the light of day when the authors thought: what better partnership for a book on beginning dressage than one experienced professional and one real live beginner?

Kathryn Denby-Wrightson
Hollis, New Hampshire

Joan Fry
Rancho Santa Fe, California

Introduction

It's a beautiful day for a ride.

You groom your horse, clean his hoofs, saddle and bridle him, and you're ready to go. As soon as you put your foot in the stirrup, your horse moves off. It's an annoying habit he has. He's a good horse, with a sweet disposition, but he has these funny little quirks that drive you crazy—like not standing still when you want to get on him.

Mounted at last, you move off. Your horse hasn't been out for a while and you know he'd probably enjoy a nice brisk canter, but you also know that if you let him, he's going to be hard to stop. Another of his little quirks. He's generally obedient, and has no really *bad* vices—just these funny habits that aren't so funny on days like this, because you'd enjoy a canter, too.

So you compromise, and let him trot.

And for a minute, it's fun. It's more than fun. For a minute, your horse is moving under you so smoothly that the two of you feel like you're moving together, with one mind and one body, and you feel a surge of exhilaration.

Then your horse starts trying to go faster. He doesn't respond to the bit—the more you try to hold him in, the higher he pokes his nose out. His backbone feels as stiff as a board and he's throwing you so high out of the saddle you're surprised it's still under you when you come down.

Oops, almost missed the trail. You try to turn your horse but he would much rather keep trotting down the field with

5

his head bent one way and his body going another. Some of the happiness you felt a minute ago starts ebbing out of you. Why won't your horse behave any better? You haul on the reins and give him a kick, and grudgingly, still fighting your hands, he comes around.

The trail is a little muddy because the sun doesn't reach here. You bring your horse down to a walk; you don't want him to slip. Immediately he loses all interest in the ride. He walks slower and slower (what he really wants to do is turn around and go home) and you feel yourself getting more and more annoyed with him, urging him on with your heels just to make sure he's not falling asleep.

But it's a losing battle. So you let him amble on at his own speed and try to enjoy yourself. If only your horse . . .

Suddenly your horse shies. He slips in the mud and almost loses his footing. With a terrific scramble he recovers himself, but you've lost both stirrups and your heart's in your mouth. What was *that* all about?

From the base of a tree comes an accusing, high-pitched chatter: a squirrel. Your horse shied at a squirrel.

He's tense now, grinding his teeth and oblivious to all your nudgings and urgings. You're as tense as he is. Your good mood has evaporated. Is it worth it to keep on going? you wonder glumly. Will riding your horse ever be as satisfying as the idea of it that you have in your mind? Isn't there *anything* you can do to help him?

There is. It's a training method that anyone can learn, and that can be taught to any horse. It's called dressage.

Some people are put off by dressage because they think it's pretty but useless—something only rich people do on fancy horses.

Not true. An equitation term from the French that means "training," dressage develops a horse's natural abilities—the way he moves and **balances*** himself. It encourages the

---

* All **boldfaced** terms are defined alphabetically in the glossary.

horse to use his **hindquarters** farther under his body and to lighten his **forehand.** When the horse begins moving **forward** with **rhythm** and **impulsion** he'll start seeking contact with the rider's hands. He will *flex* at the poll and carry his head more or less perpendicular to the ground. In any movement along a straight line the horse will be absolutely **straight;** when he turns a corner or moves along a circle he will bend to the circle throughout his entire body. Such a horse will seat his rider comfortably at *any* **gait** and is easily controlled under any circumstance, because he's physically conditioned, relaxed, and in harmony with his rider. A horse trained in dressage has an elegance that makes him not only a joy to ride but a pleasure to look at—and the quality that will strike an observer most forcefully is the ease and brilliance of the horse's movements. The horse appears to be doing of his own free will whatever his rider asks of him.

How does dressage accomplish all this?

By educating the rider so he can educate his horse. Anyone who can ride can ride dressage—and if you can afford your own horse you can afford dressage. It's not only for rich folks. By the same token, dressage isn't only for pampered, pedigreed horses. It doesn't matter if your horse is a Sunday jumper or an Appaloosa or a 12-year-old grade gelding you ride on the trail. *Any* type of horse will benefit from dressage.* There are no size, age, sex, or breed restrictions, even in formal competition.

But dressage isn't magic. It takes a lot of patience to train a horse and do a good job of it, and as one early Greek

* The head coach of the USET jumping squad teaches dressage to all the team jumpers, and hunter-jumper trainers on both coasts routinely use dressage techniques in their training. So do many top Saddlebred trainers. Magazines such as *Western Horseman* frequently run articles on how dressage can help the Western horse do everything from running barrels to competing in endurance rides.

equestrian observed, "He cannot master a horse who has not mastered himself."

I will assume for the purposes of this book that you can ride, and by "ride" I mean that you can get on your horse and stay on through the various gaits, whether you do it saddle seat, bareback, or by the skin of your teeth. I will also assume that your horse is accustomed to a bit, a saddle, and to being led and ridden. I won't be dealing with unbroken horses.

Now I'm going to take both you and your horse back to the beginning. I'm going to teach you how to develop yourself into a confident, accomplished rider, and how to develop your horse into one that's mannerly, free-moving, and a joy to ride. I'm going to show you, through photographs and easy-to-follow intructions, what to do to reach your goal of one-ness with your horse, and how it should look and feel *to you* every step of the way.

The Beginning Dressage Book is divided into three main sections, which correspond to the three main stages of training: lunging, straightforward riding, and advanced work.

The primary purpose of lunging is to make life easier for you when you get on your horse to ride. Lunging will relax the horse and improve his physical coordination. He'll learn to balance himself at the **walk, trot,** and **canter** in a circle before he's reintroduced to your weight in the saddle.

The second stage is straightforward riding. You will work together with your horse to build on what he has learned on the lunge. You learn to use your natural **aids** to achieve a secure, balanced **seat**—no more lost stirrups—to encourage the horse to move straight forward with relaxed back muscles, and to make his **transitions** from one gait to another calmly and easily.

In the third stage, you'll begin using subtler, more refined aids to get additional **engagement** and impulsion, which is the prerequisite for all further work—putting your horse **on the bit,** and gymnasticising your horse. Through progressively more demanding exercises such as the **serpentine,** the **half-halt,** and the **leg-yield,** you'll develop your horse's natural athletic abilities and his obedience to your aids until he moves forward with ease and **cadence,** without **resisting** you in any way.

Don't forget that dressage isn't an end in itself, unless you have big plans for the Olympics. It's the means to an end—the end being a superbly conditioned, relaxed, elegant riding horse. *The Beginning Dressage Book* presents one person's training methods which will achieve that end. If you do decide to compete, you'll come into contact with methods of training other than the ones I've presented in this book. Don't automatically decide that because they're different, they're wrong. Think about them, try what seems logical, and use what works. One of the hallmarks of the true horseman is that he's always learning.

You might also find that other competitors are learning from you.

But competing is far in the future. The basic purpose of *The Beginning Dressage Book* is to show you what beginning dressage is all about by explaining, step by step, how to get there.

Part One
TACK

1
Horse Equipment

If you're reading this book, you probably have a horse. And if you have a horse, you probably have a saddle and bridle. You may find that you'll be able to use the tack you already own for dressage, and by that I mean it won't be necessary to go out and buy your horse a whole new "dressage outfit."* I'm going to go over what you need in some detail, however, because to get the best results you should have the proper equipment. It's that simple.

You will need an English bridle; that is, one with a nose-band and a browband. You can't use a Western bridle for what you're going to do. The bridle can be new or used. If you have a chance to buy a good, used bridle that fits your horse, do so. Even if the throatlatch, for instance, is worn, or too short, you'll still save money in the long run if you buy it. Just have somebody who does leather repairs replace the worn throatlatch.

Always make sure that you can take an item of tack home and fit it on your horse before you buy it, or that you can return it if it doesn't fit. Most tack shops will let you do this without question.

As you probably know, bridles come in three standard sizes: pony, which is suitable for ponies up to approximately 14 hands; cob, for horses up to approximately 16 hands; and full-size, for larger horses. Most Thoroughbreds, Arabs, and

* Unless you plan to compete. I'll deal with competition tack and clothing in Part Five.

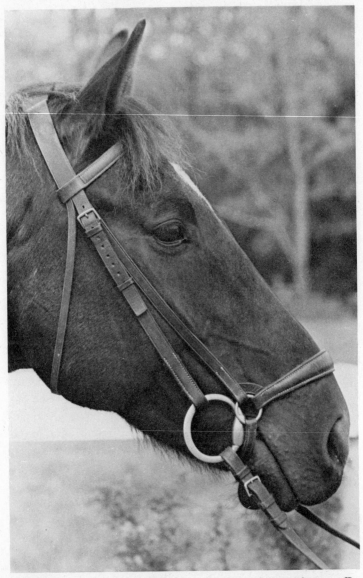

An English bridle with a dropped noseband and an eggbutt snaffle. (*Photo by George Wrightson.*)

An English bridle with a regular cavesson noseband and full-cheek snaffle. The hand between the jawbone and throatlatch indicates how tight the throatlatch should be. (*Photo by Joan Fry.*)

Quarter Horses will take a cob size. These sizes are only approximate, however, and you might find that your horse is an exception—some horses are small-boned but have big heads.

When you're fitting the bridle on your horse, remember that the browband should lie below the base of the horse's ears without pinching them, and should be long enough so that it doesn't interfere with the hang of the cheekpieces. The cheekpieces should lie a little to the front of a line drawn from the horse's lips to his ears.

Make sure the throatlatch isn't too tight. Always do up the throatlatch so that you can insert the width of your hand—all five fingers held sideways—between it and the horse's jawbone. If it's any tighter, it will interfere with your horse's breathing and his ability to flex correctly from the poll.

An ordinary noseband, or cavesson, should be halfway between the horse's projecting cheekbones and the corners of his mouth, and not over the cartilage of his nose. Fasten the cavesson *under* the cheekpieces of the bridle, and do it up loosely enough so that the horse can still open his mouth to accept a treat, such as a piece of carrot. You should be able to get two fingers, held sideways, between the noseband and the horse's face. If you have a problem with your horse opening his mouth when you ride, fasten the noseband more tightly.

If your horse is constantly opening his mouth or crossing his jaws, or gets his tongue over the bit, I recommend a dropped noseband. It's called a dropped noseband because it fits lower on the horse's nose than an ordinary cavesson. I use one with all my horses simply as a preventive measure. Be sure to fasten the part that actually goes over the horse's nose well above his nostrils; you want him to be able to breathe. The chin strap is fastened in the horse's chin groove, in *front* of the bit. Be sure to fasten it quite snugly. The noseband will fit properly if it has been sewn into a spiked ring or sewn to the cheekpiece by a strip of leather.

Never use a dropped noseband with anything except a snaffle bit.

I'm not going to go into the subject of double bridles at all. Although they have a place in dressage, you'll get the best results for what you're trying to accomplish by using a simple snaffle bridle.

The most important part of the bridle is the bit, and here

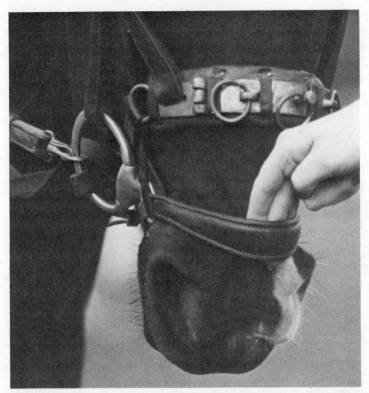

The horse tacked up with a bridle and lunging cavesson. The finger through the dropped noseband indicates how tightly to do it up. (*Photo by John Havey.*)

I'm going to be quite specific. There are hundreds of types of bits on the market, but the only kind you'll need is a smooth, jointed snaffle. As with any bit, you must select and fit a snaffle very carefully for the best results. Your horse must be taught to accept the bit, and he won't do it unless it fits him correctly. If you're using a bit that's uncomfortable for him, or too severe, he'll pull and fuss and give you a miserable ride.

Your first consideration is the proper size. Most horses that take a cob-size bridle will take a 5″ or a 5½″ bit. The correct thickness is equally important. The bit shouldn't be so thin that it pinches the horse's lips, or so thick that it's not resting properly on the bars of the mouth. Keep in mind that the thinner the bit, the stronger the effect it will have on the horse's mouth; in other words, the harsher it will be. Most horses have fairly sensitive mouths, and I recommend that you start with the thickest bit your horse can accommodate. You can get a good thickness in either an Irish- or a German-made snaffle. If your horse has a hard mouth (or a small mouth), a thinner bit will probably work better.

Both the full-cheek snaffle and the eggbutt snaffle are good because they're "quiet" in the horse's mouth. You can't pull a full-cheek snaffle sideways through the horse's mouth, and the cheeks prevent the bit from rubbing. The rings of an eggbutt snaffle are joined directly to the mouthpiece, a feature which makes this bit less likely to pinch the horse's lips than other snaffles.

There are also half-moon or straight bar (unjointed) snaffles made of vulcanite, rubber, or metal, which are very mild and can be used on horses with injured mouths. Other than that, when I say "snaffle bit," I mean a smooth, jointed snaffle. It's wrong to use any other type of bit in an effort to improve your horse's behavior. If you think your horse isn't coming along properly, it usually means that you, the rider, aren't doing your part to help your horse's training.

In my experience, stainless steel bits wear the best. They're also the most expensive. There are also nickle bits, which have a greenish look and tend to bend. Plated metal bits are inclined to flake, and unless you smooth them with steel wool, or sand the plating off completely before putting them in the horse's mouth, they will cause sores and cuts. (And after the plating has flaked off, they'll rust.)

Once you've selected a snaffle, take it home and fasten it to the bridle so that the hinge of the mouthpiece faces toward the front of the horse's mouth. A snaffle acts on the bars of the horse's mouth, that area of his lower jaw where he doesn't have any teeth. Adjust the cheekpieces of the bridle so that the bit fits comfortably on the bars without wrinkling the corners of the horse's lips more than two wrinkles. Any more than that and it's too high. If his lips don't wrinkle at all the bit is too low, and will bang around in his mouth and hurt him.

There are numerous types of reins to choose from. I suggest that you buy plain leather reins of a width that fits the size of your hand and feels comfortable to you. Braided reins look nice, but they're difficult to keep clean, and if you get the kind with laces, the lacing will break and you'll spend a lot of time trying to find somebody to repair them. If you buy used reins, be sure to cheek for loose stitching and cracks where they fasten onto the rings of the bit.

When you go shopping for tack, you'll see a lot of items on display promising short cuts or "proven results." My recommendation is to stay away from them. I'm not even going to discuss them. It can generally be said that the less tack, the better the rider. All gimmicks and gadgets are either for the circus performer or the amateur who doesn't know any better.

Well-made and correctly fitted tack adds immeasurably to the comfort and appearance of both you and your horse. Good tack is made of good leather, and it's going to cost good money. The best tack is made in Europe, and in the long run it's well worth the initial outlay. If you buy cheap tack, you'll find that it never fits quite right—it stretches and it won't last very long. Some foreign-made tack is of such poor, paper-thin leather that it's just not safe. I suggest to my students that they keep an eye out for good-quality used tack. Some riders even prefer used tack—especially saddles—so they can save themselves the bother of breaking it in.

You will need either a dressage or an all-purpose saddle. You've probably realized by now that you can't use a Western saddle for learning dressage; neither can you use a forward seat jumping saddle, or a straight-cut saddle used for riding gaited horses. All of them will put you in the wrong position on the horse for dressage.

There are many fine saddles on the market today. In general, a new saddle is best, because it will adapt to your horse's conformation and also, to a certain extent, to yours. A saddle that has been broken in by somebody else has been molded to that horse and that rider. But if you can't afford a good new saddle—and I can't stress this strongly enough—buy a good second-hand saddle rather than a cheap new one. If you hunt around diligently enough, you should be able to find a second-hand saddle made by a reputable firm that still has a lot of wear left in it. It's not an exaggeration to say that a well-made saddle, properly taken care of, will last you a lifetime.

English saddles are measured from the nailhead alongside the pommel to the highest point of the cantle. To find out how many inches that is, run a tape measure from the nail to the cantle, and pull it tight. Don't measure the dip of the seat. Sizes vary somewhat from manufacturer to manufacturer, but on the average, a woman of medium height and build will take a 17″ or a 17½″ saddle, a teenager will take a 16″, and an average-size man will take an 18″ or a 19″.

It's difficult to describe how a dressage or all-purpose saddle should fit you, especially if you're used to riding some other way. As a rider, one of your main objectives in dressage will be to achieve an independent seat, firmly balanced, deep in the lowest part of the saddle, with your legs fairly long. Dressage saddles have longer, straighter flaps than most other types in order to give you the maximum amount of help in maintaining a balanced seat. You'll be able to "feel" your seat in a dressage saddle almost immediately.

All-purpose saddles, which can be used for jumping and cross-country riding as well as for dressage, generally have knee-rolls to help keep your legs in position while you jump.

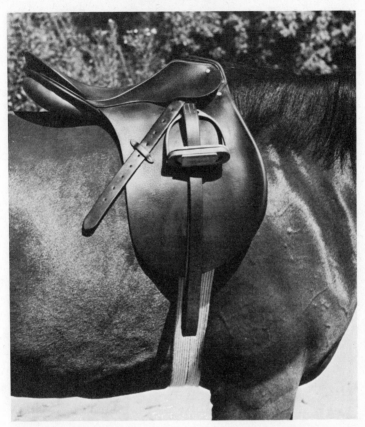

A dressage saddle. The saddle is a little too far forward. (*Photo by Joan Fry.*)

Even in expensive saddles the knee-rolls sometimes have too much stuffing in them or else the stuffing is in the wrong place, which will result in a loss of contact with the horse and will force you into adopting an incorrect seat. All-purpose saddles can give you a more comfortable ride over long periods of time on the trail than dressage saddles, but they also tend to push you into more of a forward seat position.

The width of your horse's back will determine whether you need a saddle with a wide, narrow, or medium tree, and

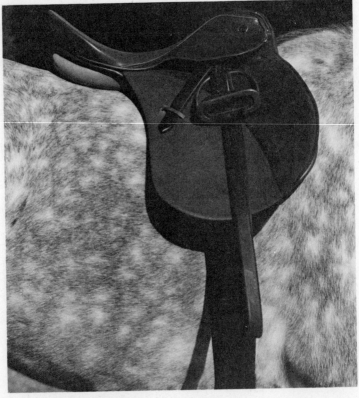

An all-purpose saddle. (*Photo by Joan Fry.*)

you can pretty well judge this for yourself by looking at how sharply your horse's sides slope away from his backbone. The tree is made of wood, generally beechwood, and is the main supporting structure of your saddle—and wood will split if you're careless about how you treat your saddle. (A saddle with a broken tree is not always visible to the untrained eye, so be especially careful if you're shopping for a used saddle.)

I strongly advise you to take a trainer or other knowledgeable person with you when you shop for tack, especially saddles. He or she will be able to help you make the initial selection, and when you take the saddle home to fit it, he can tell whether you've gotten the proper size for your weight and build and whether the saddle fits your horse. When you put the saddle on your horse's back, *make sure* there's no weight on his loins, and no pressure at all on his spine. If there is, the tree is too wide for his back and he'll get sore. Have your trainer look closely at how the saddle rests on the horse's back after you're mounted. You must be absolutely certain that the saddle rests evenly on the lumbar muscles on either side of the horse's spine, and that your weight isn't pressing the saddle against his backbone. Also make sure that the saddle doesn't rub on the horse's withers or inhibit his ability to move his shoulders. Be especially careful about this last point if you're trying out an all-purpose saddle with knee-rolls.

Unfortunately, there are no hard and fast rules about how a saddle should fit you, or how many fingers, hands, etc., you should be able to fit between the horse's withers and the underside of the pommel. These factors will vary from saddle to saddle. My own experience has been that French- or German-made dressage or all-purpose saddles suit me best.

Don't use a saddle without a saddle pad. Saddle pads aren't for padding—they're to keep your saddle from getting dirty. You want the thinnest pad you can get so that you're still in contact with your horse's back. The best pads are made of felt or sheepskin. You can dry a felt pad and then brush it hard with a dandy brush to get the dirt out. Sheepskin pads are washable—using pure wool soap and a scrub brush. Stay away from the thick, wooly, man-made pads that look like sheepskin but aren't. These will put too much padding between you and the horse. The inexpensive, lightweight, quilted cotton pads are also very good. (You can make your own out of a cotton mattress pad.) I don't recommend leather pads because they tend to rub the horse's back. Make sure that if you have an all-purpose saddle you get an all-purpose pad, and if you have a dressage saddle that you get a dressage pad, because the cuts are different. The saddle pad should be larger than the saddle by about one inch all the way around. And when you fit it on the horse, especially if it's one of the soft, yielding variety, make sure that you tuck up the front part into the underside of the pommel; otherwise, it will stretch tight across the horse's withers and rub.

Girths, like bits, are sold by the inch. When measuring your horse for the first time, put the saddle on his back. Counting from the third hole from the bottom of the billet strap, measure the horse's belly to the third hole from the bottom of the billet strap on the other side. How many inches you get is the size of the girth you want. There are many different types of girth, and they come in all kinds of colors. Be discreet. No matter how stylish you think your horse would look in a sunshine yellow girth, stick to white. String girths are generally good and easy to keep clean, although they tend to shrink with washing. They're less likely to slip than other kinds, and since they allow air to pass through to the horse's sides they're also less likely to rub. I use them more for competing than for everyday riding. Nylon girths are similar to string, but they slip a little more and, when they're new, they stretch. I don't recommend web girths because they don't last very long and they tend to come apart unexpectedly. The best girths are leather. They come either full leather or with elastic on the ends, which makes them a little more adjustable than full leather. There are also several different cuts. My personal favorite is the three-fold, because if you keep a well-oiled strip of cloth between the folds, the whole girth will stay soft and pliable. (If you buy a three-fold, fasten it so that the crease is toward the horse's front legs; otherwise, it can chafe.)

Your stirrup irons should be of the best quality you can afford. Steel or stainless steel are the nicest-looking and also the safest. Plated metal iron stirrups, like plated metal bits, flake off. (You can counteract this to a certain extent by painting the entire stirrup iron with lacquer or clear varnish.) I don't recommend safety stirrups, which have elastic on one side. They're unnecessary for what you'll be doing. Offset stirrups are used mainly by people who ride hunters and jumpers using a forward seat saddle, and I don't recommend them either.

Some riders like the security of rubber stirrup treads. These help keep your feet in the correct position and lessen the chance of your heel sliding completely through the stirrup iron. I think these are definitely worthwhile, and I always advise my students to invest in them. The stirrup iron should fit your boot so that you have half an inch on either side of the widest part of your boot. If you leave more space, you're inviting the risk of your heel sliding through.

To find the length of stirrup leather you need, measure the length from the middle joint of your third finger to your armpit and multiply by three. All stirrup leathers will stretch a little once you begin using them. Cheap ones will break. If you buy used stirrup leathers, check carefully for loose stitching and cracks.

Take care of your tack. Rinse the bit with water and clean your saddle and bridle with a little saddle soap and lukewarm water every time you ride. When you're finished riding, put your tack away properly, so that it has a chance to air out. Nothing in the world smells quite as unappetizing as an old, dirty, sweaty saddle pad that you've thrown into a corner someplace and forgotten about. Inspect your tack periodically to see how the stitching is holding up, and whether it needs oiling. Check that your bit hasn't developed any burrs or worn spots; check that your girth is holding together and that your reins and stirrup leathers are pliable and haven't dried out. All leather will dry and eventually crack unless you replace the natural oil. Neatsfoot oil, glycerin, caster oil, olive oil—almost any unsalted animal or vegetable oil is good. (The exceptions are linseed oil and mineral oil, which will harden leather.) Be sure to work it into the leather well—you want the oil on your saddle, not on the seat of your riding pants.

You're probably already familiar with most of the items of tack I've just gone over, since their use isn't confined to dressage. But you will need a few items specifically for your work in dressage. In some cases you can improvise; in others, you'll just have to grit your teeth and hand over your money.

You'll need a proper dressage whip, one that's at least 36″ long. Other types of whips, such as hunting crops or Western bats, are much too short, and you'll have to take your hands off the reins in order to use them correctly.

If your horse is at all lethargic you might need spurs, but I strongly suggest that you try to ride using a whip and your legs. If you find that you do need spurs, get the very short, blunt type called Prince of Wales spurs. These are very easy on a horse, because no matter what you do with your legs you won't gouge his sides. On no account use spurs with rowels in them. You can buy very beautiful and elegant stainless steel dressage spurs, which have got long shanks on them, but I don't recommend these for beginning riders. It's too easy to inadvertently kill the feeling in a horse's sides with them.

You'll need a lunge whip so that you can work your horse from the ground. You should be able to reach him with the lash end of the lunge whip from where you're standing without walking up to him. Since your beginning work on the lunge will be done on a circle with a radius of at least 20 feet (the distance between you and the horse), you'll find that most lunge whips aren't nearly long enough. I suggest to my students that they buy a couple of 36″ or 48″ leather bootlaces and tie them to the end of the lash. My lunge whip measures 11′ from stock to lash end, and by adding two bootlaces I've increased the length to nearly 20 feet.

You'll also need a lunge line. The one I have is 40 feet long, and there are times when I need that extra length because one of my horses is a very young, active, foolish horse. You probably won't need one longer than 20 feet, but don't get anything shorter than that. I prefer a web lunge line, although they do cost more than the lightweight nylon ones. The latter tend to sail off in the breeze while you're working your horse, and you'll find it very difficult to feel what kind of contact you have with him through the lunge line. If you don't have a proper lunge line, you can improvise with clothesline or any fairly heavy rope or cord.

You can't lunge a horse and expect to teach him anything unless you've got a lunging cavesson. This is a type of headgear that resembles the headstall of a bridle or halter except that it fits very snugly and has a ring in the center of the noseband where the lunge line is fastened. I don't recommend a halter for lunging. It doesn't fit snugly enough, and no matter where you attach the lunge line, you'll end up pulling the whole halter around on the horse's face, distracting him and interfering with his way of going. Don't be tempted to attach the lunge line to the noseband of the bridle, and *never* attach it to the rings of the bit. You can pull the entire bit right through the horse's mouth that way. A cavesson will give you all the control you need, and is the most effective way of getting the results you want. An old-fashioned leather-and-brass cavesson is a very expensive piece of equipment. Lately, however, manufacturers have come up with nylon lunging cavessons that are every bit as good as the leather ones and considerably cheaper.

It would be nice if you could afford a surcingle (also known as a belly band or a roller), but it's not crucial. A surcingle is a wide piece of leather, like a girth, that encircles the horse's back and stomach. It has rings in it for fastening lines, and you can use it instead of a saddle for lunging.

Side reins, on the other hand, *are* crucial to a horse's training, but you must use them properly or you'll defeat your whole purpose. Side reins are essentially two long lines, one on either side of the horse's neck, that you attach from

The horse with a lunging cavesson only, to indicate how snug the cavesson should be. (*Photo by John Havey.*)

the bit to the saddle or surcingle. If you don't have side reins, you can use leather straps. I would rather you use leather than cord because leather is less likely to stretch and you can be more certain of getting both pieces the same length. I'll discuss the use and adjustment of side reins in greater detail in the chapters on lunging, but I want to stress here that you aren't using side reins to artificially "set" your horse's head. The only purpose of side reins in lunging is to help the horse step into the tracks of his front feet with his hind feet. They'll stop the snaky, uncertain movements horses tend to make when they're first learning to lunge.

There are a few other items of tack that may be helpful in your horse's training but which probably won't be necessary. What I have in mind are leg wraps and the various kinds of boots, which are all used as precautionary measures in schooling young horses or horses that aren't used to working on a lunge line. Most furnish support for the tendons of the front legs. Unless your horse interferes with himself, you won't need boots or wraps for his hind legs. If you know how to do it, you can wrap your horse's front legs with wraps and cotton. If you don't know how, use shin boots. If your horse is young and uncoordinated, you may find that he cuts his front heels with his hind feet once you start work on the lunge line. Get him a pair of galloping boots—round, bell-shaped boots that fasten around the horse's front hoofs and prevent him from hurting himself. But, once again, most of these boots and wraps are only precautionary measures, and unless your horse actually needs them, there's no reason for you to spend money on them. Save up for a good pair of riding boots instead.

2
The Rider's Dress

What you should wear when you school your horse depends, with only a few exceptions, on what you already own. I would like to emphasize one thing, however. If you have any thoughts, any little inklings, that you might someday wish to compete, I would advise you to wear clothes as similar as possible to what's required in formal dressage competition. The first time you compete you're going to be nervous enough without having to cope with a completely new suit of clothes. You'll feel like a man in a tuxedo for the first time in his life—it's new and it's stiff and it's not one bit comfortable. But if you've worn those clothes while you've been training your horse, they'll feel as friendly and well-worn as an old pair of shoes.

The suggestions that follow are mainly for your comfort and safety.

I do recommend a hard hat, such as the kind hunter-jumper people wear. If you can't afford a hard hat, try to get some kind of protective helmet, even a motorcycle helmet, and make sure that it fits you properly. Even the most polished rider can fall off a horse and land head first, so buy a hard hat and save yourself some headaches.

I always tell my students to wear a shirt or blouse with a stiff collar. Once you begin to train your horse from the saddle and are working on a balanced seat, you'll be able to use the collar as a guide for your backbone. And if you're fortunate enough to have a teacher, or someone on the ground to help you, it will be much easier for that person to see the position of your back, shoulders, and arms if you're wearing a shirt or blouse than if you're wearing a sweatshirt or something else that's bulky and shapeless. And tuck in your shirt. If you wear it outside your pants, it will balloon out in back and you'll look like the Hunchback of Notre Dame no matter how you're sitting.

I'd like you to wear gloves. You should always wear them in competition, and even if you never compete, they'll save a lot of wear and tear on your hands. I suggest fairly heavy, durable leather gloves, not dress gloves. If you can't afford leather, a very good and inexpensive substitute, available at any hardware store, is vinyl gardening gloves. I use them for riding, for grooming my horse, for cleaning my tack, and (surprise!) for gardening.

I also suggest proper riding pants. As you read this, you may be envisioning the old-fashioned jodhpurs with the bulges at the sides that looked like the flotilla pontoons used to keep boats up out of the water. Riding pants don't look like that nowadays. They're very snug and trim and fit right to your leg from ankle to waist. They're usually made of stretch material of some kind that gives with the movement of your leg, and they're very comfortable to ride in.

Jodhpurs are cuffed and worn over short boots. Riding breeches are shorter in the legs, are not cuffed, and go under knee-length boots. If you don't have riding pants, a pair of jeans will do, although I personally find jeans very uncomfortable. The seams down the inside invariably rub my legs raw. Most jeans also fit too loose in the leg (and if they fit you the way they're supposed to you'll probably split them when you try to mount) and will ride up on your leg and twist around as you rise to the trot. If you do use jeans, use an old beat-up pair, preferably straight-legged (peg-legged are even better, if you can find them), and take in the seam around the ankles. If you're not big on sewing, fold the legs of your jeans over to the outside of your leg, away from the saddle, and pull a pair of long, heavy socks on over them. Or, take an Ace bandage (or one of your horse's leg bandages) and wrap your legs from the knee down, over your jeans. The bandage will hold the legs of your jeans in place and keep them snug.

It's possible to ride in almost any kind of boot or sturdy shoe, and riding in hiking boots has become quite a fad in certain parts of the country. Whatever kind of boot you wear, *make sure* that it has a good, substantial heel. Without one you run the risk of having your entire foot slide through the stirrup if the horse shies or does something unexpected. Unless you can get your foot out of that stirrup, you're in trouble.

I don't suggest wearing cowboy boots—they're too short. As you ride up and down at the trot, the tops will catch under the flaps of the saddle and you'll have to keep reaching down and moving the flap away from your leg. I recommend either short, ankle-length boots or the classic knee-length English riding boots. I've suggested black rubber boots to a lot of my students who couldn't afford leather boots. They last forever, and you can muck out stalls in them and wear them in any kind of weather. You can even compete in them. Their only drawback is that they make your feet perspire. (My mother used to tell me that horses sweat, men perspire, and ladies glow. If you're a lady, resign yourself to the fact that rubber boots will give you glowing feet.) Although good leather riding boots are expensive, I suggest you start saving your pennies and buy a pair as soon as you can afford them. They make all the difference in the world. They feel better, they have a stronger effect on the horse's sides, and they give a better line to your leg. And don't forget to look into second-hand boots. You can often find used riding boots in some unlikely places, such as church rummage sales.

Take care of your boots the same way you take care of your leather tack. If you let your boots go without periodic cleaning and oiling, the leather will crease and harden and chafe your feet. You can help keep your boots from creasing at the ankles by using boot trees, or stuffing rolled newspapers into the leg. Properly taken care of, leather boots will give you hours of riding pleasure and last a long time.

Part Two
TRAINING FROM THE GROUND–LUNGING

3
Introduction to Lunging

Training your horse from the saddle will be much easier if you get to know each other on the lunge line first. You'll learn about your horse's temperament and idiosyncrasies, how his muscles work—especially the muscles of his back and hindquarters—and the sequence and rhythm of the individual steps he takes at the walk, trot, and canter. The horse, in turn, will get to know you, which is important, because he won't learn if he's afraid of you or doesn't trust you.

Lunging is your first step in getting the horse fit. Lunging will develop his muscles, give balance and a steady rhythm to his gaits, and help him with his head and neck carriage. It's also a way of exercising your horse if you can't ride him for one reason or another.

Athletes always do warm-up exercises before getting down to serious business, and you can limber your horse up the same way by lunging him. Also, if you mount a well-rested horse, even one that's not particularly hot-blooded, he's probably going to act up. By lunging him first, you can get all the little kinks out and make sure he's ready to go to work.

If somebody's willing to lunge your horse while you ride him, lunging will teach you how to sit properly. Before you can help your horse engage his hindquarters, you must have what is called an independent seat. In other words, your seat must be independent of your hands, arms, legs—every other

37

part of your body. If somebody else is lunging your horse, you have an excellent opportunity to concentrate on your position in the saddle. I won't be dealing with the rider's seat until Part Three, and if you do have a friend who's willing to lunge your horses while you ride, I urge you to reread that entire section before you start.

Your immediate goal in lunging is to develop a happy, obedient, rhythmic, and balanced horse. First you're going to relax him and give him confidence in you. Then you're going to work on the rhythm of his strides and on keeping him straight and moving forward, which will give him balance. Engagement and impulsion will result from balance.

In the beginning, your aids on the lunge line will be very direct. As your horse begins to understand what you want, your aids will become much more subtle. When you start riding, you'll notice the same progression, until eventually your horse will need only a very light aid to tell him what to do. You can achieve a remarkable degree of balance through lunging once your horse accepts your hands through the lunge line.

For those of you unfamiliar with English tack, let me briefly go over the correct way to saddle and bridle a horse in order to lunge him.

Saddle him while he still has his halter on. Lower the saddle gently on top of his withers and slide it back (in the direction his hair grows) to approximately an inch behind his withers. The actual distance isn't important; what you must make sure of is that the knee-roll area of the saddle completely clears the horse's shoulders and allows them to move without constraint. Pull the horse's mane out from under the gullet of the saddle. You don't need to do up the girth too tightly because you won't be getting on, but make sure it's secure enough so that the saddle doesn't slip. Either run up the stirrup irons or take them off completely. Later on, as your horse gets used to the equipment, you can let them dangle.

The horse tacked up with a bit, bridle, and lunging cavesson. (*Photo by John Havey.*)

Next, take off the halter and bridle him. Slip the reins over his head as though you were getting on to ride, so that if he tries to walk off, you have something to hold on to. Then reach your right hand under the horse's head and around to the other side so that your hand is just over his nostrils. Take hold of the bridle about halfway down the cheekpieces with that same hand and hold it there, just above his nose. Slip the bit between the thumb and index fingers of your left hand and bring it up under the horse's mouth. The horse should open his mouth and accept it. If he

Criss-crossing the reins under the horse's jaw. (*Photo by John Havey.*)

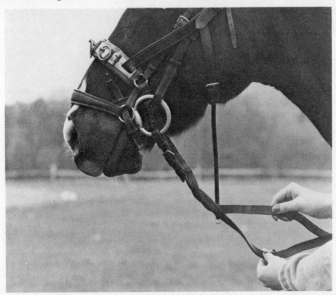

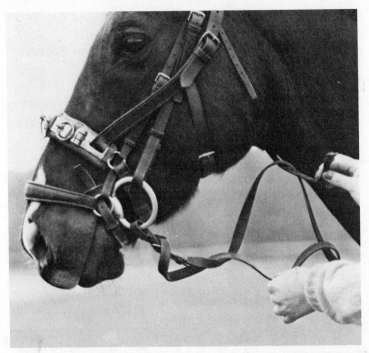

Criss-crossing the reins under the horse's jaw. (*Photo by John Havey.*)

has his teeth clenched, don't try to force the bit in—you will only bump his gums and teeth and make him even more reluctant to be bridled. If he won't open his mouth, gradually bring your left hand up so that the bit is against his teeth. Wiggle your forefinger between his lips where there's a gap between his teeth on the far side. On the near side use your thumb. Press down against his gums with both fingers. The horse will open his mouth. Slide the bit in without bumping him and slip the bridle over his ears with your right hand.

The lunging cavesson fits over the bridle, but make sure that you fasten the noseband *under* the cheekpieces of the bridle. The whole cavesson has to be quite snug, and this is the only time I can think of when you disregard the general rule of thumb about fitting a headstall on a horse. If the cavesson is too loose, it's going to slide around on the horse's head and chafe and distract him.

Making sure that the bridle reins are still over the horse's neck in a normal riding position, take hold of the reins under the horse's throat, one rein in each hand, and cross them. Cross them again. Criss-cross them a few more times and then pass the throatlatch through *one* of them and do up the throatlatch. This arrangement will keep your reins from getting in the way of the horse's legs.

Now connect your side reins. Attach them to the saddle by running them through one of the billets fastening the girth to the saddle. When the horse is standing calmly with his head and neck in a very natural, relaxed position, fasten the side reins to the rings of the snaffle above the bridle reins. Make sure that the side reins are long enough so that they have no real effect on the horse's head carriage. Don't ever attempt to "set" your horse's head by pushing his nose in before you fasten the side reins. He'll acquire the proper flexion at the poll with more muscling and more impulsion from the hindquarters as his schooling progresses. You can't do it artificially.

In all stages of training it's important not to worry or scare your horse, so your next step is to introduce him to the lunge whip and the lunge line by letting him look at them and smell them. If you have a hot-blooded horse that tends to blow up at new things, this might take a few minutes. Take your time. Talk to him. Run your whip over his body, using the end that you hold in your hand. Run it over his neck, around his face, up and down his legs, through his legs, under his belly, over his back, around his hindquarters, under his tail. Don't start doing anything on the lunge line until your horse stands quietly and without fear while you touch him all over with both the lunge line and the whip.

Now fasten your lunge line to the center ring on the cavesson and lead the horse to where you're going to lunge him. For your sake, I hope it's an enclosed area, so that he's not

The horse completely tacked up and ready to lunge. The side reins are correctly adjusted. (*Photo by John Havey.*)

going to be tempted to run off. If you don't have a ring, use some kind of fenced area, such as a pasture, where you can use two sides of a fence. The horse will think he's in an enclosure.

What comes next is a very important part of lunging: the horse's play time. (And for the sake of the discussion I'm going to assume that you're in a ring. Don't do this in a pasture.) You want your horse to be happy on the lunge. You want him energetic and free-spirited, and that means that you have to keep the training sessions from turning into drudgery for him. Before you actually get down to work, give him some time to run around. Either let the lunge line out as far as possible so that he's still under your control and won't hurt or overexert himself, or, if he's not very active by nature, let him go. (And if you just turn him loose, take off the side reins.) Encourage—not make, but encourage—the horse to kick up his heels, run, gallop, buck, do whatever he wants to. You should stand as quietly as possible, without moving. As you and your horse get to know each other better, even if he's quite young, you can simply turn him loose in the ring and let him play all he wants to. I've found that, especially with horses kept in a stall most of the time, this is really the only "fun" they have. It would be exactly the same situation if you were cooped up in a room all day long without a chance to stretch your legs. The horse feels the same way—he gets bored too.

After a week or two you'll find that your horse knows he's going to be let out and encouraged to play, and that he'll really exert himself and make full use of every minute. This is good for him psychologically, because he'll associate his training session with his play time, and he'll associate them both with his trainer—you—coming to take him out. He'll think training is a lot of fun, and you want him to keep thinking that.

If he's uncertain of what you want, clap your hands or cluck to him to get him started. Don't crack your lunge whip at him. Urge him on with your voice—anything you think will encourage him to run without scaring him. Once you've got him going, encourage him to make a lot of turns and to go in different directions. Don't just let him gallop around and around one way.

If your horse would rather hang over the fence and whinny to his friends instead of playing, get him moving by using your whip in a back and forth motion on the ground beside him. (A complete description of how to use your lunge whip is given in Chapter 4.) Soon, no matter how much your horse bucks and kicks up his heels during play time, you'll find that he tends to move around you in a circle.

When your horse is ready to work, he'll slow down. He won't be as willing to play and snort around. That's when you snap your lunge line to the center ring of the cavesson again and get down to business.

4
The Walk

Walk with your horse the way you would if he were on a lead rope, with the lunge line in your right hand if you're going to the right and in your left hand if you're going to the left. Your whip should be in your other hand. Walk along the fenceline to the **inside** of your horse, and don't look back at him. Talk to him. As you're walking, start teaching him a vocabulary, using the same words that you'll use when you lunge him. As you're walking, say "walk," in a low, calm tone of voice. Of course he already *is* walking, so praise him. Keep repeating the word "walk" and praising him.

You don't have to use the word "walk." You can say "cat." You can whistle. I use a clucking noise. In fact I don't use any words at all, except for "whoa." (I pronounce it "ho," and in this book that's how we'll spell it. I say it twice in a low, calm, sing-song tone of voice: "HO-ho, HO-ho.") For everything else I use a clucking noise. Most horses find this method easy to understand, and I don't have to remember to use different words and different inflections. I'm going to spell out my own method here because it might help give you a better idea of what you're trying to accomplish with your voice aid.

When I want the horse to walk, I use one quick, abrupt cluck. To ask for the trot I use three or four consecutive clucks in the rhythm of the trot, in a one-two, one-two rhythm, and I do it at a slightly higher pitch. If the horse starts speeding up, I'll say, "HO-ho, easy," in a calm, soothing voice. The horse will start coming down because he thinks he's supposed to **halt,** but just as he approaches the proper speed and tempo of the trot I start to cluck in the rhythm that I want. I cluck continuously to the horse as he's trotting so that he can hear the rhythm. To ask for a canter I use a long-drawn-out clucking sound, and it's very exaggerated. Other than talking to the horse, this clucking noise is all I use. When he's at the canter and I want him to come down to a halt, I say "HO-ho." The horse thinks he's supposed to come down to a halt, but in the process he has to come down through the trot and the walk. When he reaches the walk I say "good boy!" very enthusiastically several times. This tells the horse that's as far as I want him to come down; he doesn't have to go into a complete halt.

When you stop walking, your horse is going to stop walking too. He's used to this from being on a lead rope. Just as he's about to stop, say "HO-ho," or "halt," or whatever word you've decided to use. When he halts with you, praise him. Praise him with your voice and with good strong pats on the neck. Let him know he's done well.

Give your horse a lot of praise, and make sure he *knows* when he's being praised. When you tell him "good boy," make sure it's in a light, affectionate tone of voice. Even if you have to raise your voice a couple of octaves until you sound like a dumb blond movie star talking baby talk to her teddy bear—do it. Your horse *has* to be able to tell the difference between praise and a command. If you watch your horse's ears, you can tell he knows when he's being praised. At first this "praising tone" won't mean anything to him except that it's pleasant and it's not asking him to do anything. Then he'll begin moving his ears back and forth, one cocked forward while the other is back. He'll begin to look as though he's actually listening to what you're saying.

If you use voice aids, make sure that you use a different inflection for each different command. For instance, when you say "walk," say it slowly and in a low, deep tone of voice. It helps if you remember to use a higher tone of voice when you ask for an upward transition (from the halt to a walk, for instance) and a lower tone of voice when you ask for a downward transition (from walk to halt). When you say "HO-ho," make sure that you say it quickly, so that it comes out sounding short and rather abrupt. A horse can't tell the difference between "walk" and "halt" and "good boy" if you say them all in a monotone. He doesn't understand what the words mean; he only associates a specific sound with a specific action. This is why it's so important to use the same word or sound every time.

Now leave the fenceline and begin walking with your horse in a big circle, still asking him to stop and then walk on again, so that he's thinking and on his toes. Let's assume that you're walking in a circle counterclockwise, to your left. You have the lunge line coiled in your left hand and you're holding the whip in your right. Your upper arms should be in a relaxed, natural position from the shoulder, and your lower arms should be at right angles to them with your elbows at your sides and almost touching your waist. But don't keep your elbows glued to your sides; your arms shouldn't be stiff. Keep your upper arms straight and let your lower arms pivot freely from the elbow. Your arm and hand position on the lunge line and the whip is identical to the one you'll use from the saddle.

Gradually begin decreasing the size of *your* circle. As you slow down, keep telling the horse to "walk," and keep feeding out the lunge line, a little at a time. Then come to a complete stop, facing him. You're going to stay in the center of the circle while the horse walks around you. The first couple of times that you stop, your horse is going to want to stop too. As far as he's concerned, every time you stop, he stops. He doesn't understand that this is a new situation. Keep encouraging him to walk on by using your voice and praising him.

Stand so that you're opposite his shoulder. Some horses

The horse walking on the lunge line. The lunge line should be straight; this one is twisted from play time. (*Photo by John Havey.*)

prefer that you stand a little closer to their head and others would rather have you farther back, by their ribs. You'll have to watch your horse and see how he goes best. The one thing you must never do is stand directly in front of his head, because this will inhibit his willingness to go forward.

Once you're standing still and the horse is moving around you in a circle, you should form a triangle with your horse: your horse is the base, the lunge line is the front side of the triangle, and your whip is the other side.

Talk to your horse and encourage him to walk on. When

The triangle formed by the horse, the lunge line, and the whip. (*Photo by John Havey.*)

he has walked completely around the circle once or twice, ask him to halt. He may not understand right away, so be patient. (Think of it as a chance to build character.) Keep asking your horse to halt until he does it. If he's stopped paying attention to you, try holding your hand up close to your face, as if you were signaling for a right-hand turn. When he does stop, walk straight up to him, taking up the lunge line as you go, talking to him and telling him "good boy, good boy!"

Now, how do you get back to the center of the circle and

get him walking around you again? If you know that he'll stand still at the halt, you can try simply walking back to where you were in the center of the circle and then asking him to walk on. But if he's going to follow you, walk beside him again. Gradually work him into a circle again and gradually decrease the size of *your* circle until you're in the center and he's walking around you. You have to put yourself in the horse's place and make sure you're always one step ahead of him. You'll find that it will help a lot if you know in advance what you want to work on that day, and how you're going to ask for it.

When you first start lunging, it's generally easier if you have your horse going counterclockwise, or to his (and your) left. He's used to walking on your right side on a lead rope, so it's easier to get him going past you on the outside, which will be to your left. After he's walked around the circle a couple of times, halted, and has resumed walking again, ask him to turn around so that he's going in the opposite direction—clockwise. You do this by asking for the halt. Then walk up to him and walk him around a half-circle to his left (*into* the circle) so that he's facing in the other direction. Always ask him to halt, praise him, and then turn him in toward the center of the circle. Then go away in the opposite direction.

You never want the horse to turn out from the circle. In lunging, a horse that turns out, away from you, is difficult to control, and in your subsequent work from the saddle you will always ask the horse to turn *into* the center of the circle you're working on.

It may be difficult to get your horse going to the right. Keep trying, keep repeating your voice aid. Remember that even in these beginning steps you mustn't ask too much of your horse. He'll decide he'd rather be doing something else, and you'll be leaving yourself open to disobedience. But don't get impatient with him either. This is all new to him, and it may take a while for him to understand what you want. Going to the right may be especially hard for him. He may either want to stop or come in to you. If he decides he doesn't want to have anything more to do with this, don't punish him. This is when you use your whip aid. Walk toward him, saying "walk, *good* boy, walk," clucking and encouraging him to walk. If he still doesn't understand, point the lash end of the whip toward his nose and cluck. This will usually do the trick. If he still doesn't understand, remain quiet for a minute, and start talking to him. Then go up to him and have him walk beside you again. When he starts to walk, praise him.

Work your horse on a circle that's at least 40 feet in diameter. (Remember that the radius of the circle is the distance between you and your horse. The diameter is twice that distance.) You can physically damage a horse by working him on too small a circle, and you're going to make it harder for him to achieve balance and to bend correctly to the curve of the circle if the circle is too small. When your horse knows what you're asking and begins walking easily on the circle and knows the voice aids of "walk" and "halt" and how to change direction, then you can increase the size of the circle. Don't ask the horse to do it. You must step back away from him.

If you feel that your horse isn't under your control as much as you'd like, keep him on a shorter line. But don't forget that your horse *must* travel in a circle that's at least 40 feet in diameter. Shorten your lunge line (by walking out to the horse) until you're about 10 feet away from him. Then *you* are going to have to walk in a larger circle, because the horse must still have a circle that's 40 feet in diameter to go around on.

This is very important. If your horse is 10 feet away from you on the lunge line, it means that you have to walk in a circle that's about 30 feet in diameter. Try to take a few long

strides rather than a lot of short, hurried ones. Horses tend
to pick up speed if they see that the person lunging them is
moving quickly.

Unless you've lunged a horse before, the first few times
you try it you'll probably feel overwhelmed by paraphernalia—the lunge whip is unwieldy and keeps getting caught on
things, and you feel as though you have about 100 feet of
lunge line out. Be careful to keep it off the ground. If you
have too much slack, either the horse will get tangled up in it
or you will. Be especially careful that you don't get a loop
caught around your foot when you move away from your
horse to make a bigger circle and are paying out lunge line
as you go.

While your horse is walking around you in a circle, you
should be moving your lunge whip in a long, sweeping,
back-and-forth motion all the time, so that the horse is always aware of it. The movement will encourage him to keep
moving forward. You use the whip basically the same way
for everything you want the horse to do. The movement
begins behind the horse's tail. Sweep the lash forward, on
the ground, toward his forelegs, then sweep it back towards
his tail, on the ground. Think of the movement as holding a
small paintbrush and making the same horizontal brush
strokes on a piece of paper held some distance away from
you: back and forth, back and forth. If your horse needs a
stronger aid, let the whip trail along his side, from his flanks
to his ribs and girth. Never just poke him in the ribs with it,
and don't use it around his head or he'll get headshy. Your
horse should understand and respect the whip, not fear it,
and there's no reason for you to brandish it like a lion tamer.

If your horse refuses to settle down to a calm, steady walk,
or if he keeps trying to pull away from you, use a give-and-
take motion with your hand and wrist. The walk has four
beats, one per hoofbeat. Every second beat, "take," and
every fourth beat, "give": one-*two*-three-*four,* one-*take*-

three-*give*. It's not an abrupt and continuous pull, but a quick, supple, almost pulsating movement of your hand—similar to the way you'd squeeze a sponge. Use the give-and-take until the horse quiets down and begins moving forward in a relaxed, rhythmic manner. The give-and-take movement will help relax the horse's poll area, and you'll be able to feel a lighter contact on the lunge line.

You always want a constant, even contact through the lunge line from your horse's cavesson to your hand. This feeling is like a stretched elastic band being slowly released, but not to the point of slackness. The contact must be light and even, never strong or jerky.

Always use your whip and your lunge line together. If you use the lunge line in a give-and-take motion, you must use the whip at the same time to encourage the horse to keep moving forward. Remember that lunging is the beginning of your horse's training, and that everything in dressage builds on what has come before. Once you begin to ride, your voice will be replaced by your body in the saddle. Your lunge whip will be replaced by your legs, and the lunge line will be replaced by the reins. So using your lunge line together with your whip is like using your rein and leg aids together when you ride. The lunge whip encourages your horse to move forward with longer, more regular strides. This is ultimately what you want in any gait: long, regular, free, unconstrained strides, not short, quick, choppy ones.

When you ask for the halt, try using your voice aid at the same time that you "take" on the lunge line by making a fist until the horse comes to a stop. Then "give." What you are doing is closing the front of your triangle by "taking" with your hand on the lunge line. The horse walks into your closed hand, and stops.

Never get impatient with your horse. Make sure that he thoroughly understands each step before you take him on to the next one. Don't worry about how long it takes him to

"Give" on the lunge line. (*Photo by John Havey.*)

"Take" on the lunge line. (*Photo by John Havey.*)

learn about lunging and, above all, don't compare him with other horses. If a friend's horse takes one day to learn and understand what I've just covered, your horse may take a couple of days. He might even take a couple of weeks. It depends on the individual horse.

In the beginning, the most common problem that horses have is trying to come in to the center of the circle. The horse is especially likely to misinterpret what you want when you try to increase the size of the circle by stepping back and away from him. If he does try to turn in, move up closer to him, shortening the lunge line as you go and pointing the whip at his nose. If that doesn't work, you'll have to walk beside him again.

Don't let your horse be too finicky about lunging. If there are puddles in his ring, make him go through them. Don't let him slow down. If he tries to sidestep them, or if he likes to cut his corners, either walk backward, away from him, or shorten the lunge line to keep the same even contact.

If your horse is going too fast, use your voice aid for the halt, but at the same time keep your whip going along the ground. Tell him "HO-ho, HO-ho," using your whip simultaneously, so that he knows you don't want him to stop entirely. When he obeys, make sure to praise him.

Be sure to give your horse aids only when he needs them and never too frequently; otherwise, he'll become indifferent to them.

To keep your horse (and yourself) from getting bored, vary the exercises. There are a lot of things you can do at the walk. You can ask for the halt, you can change direction, you can ask the horse to lengthen or shorten his strides. You do this by lengthening or shortening your own strides (but still maintaining the four-beat rhythm of the walk) and aiding with the whip in longer or shorter strokes. Another thing that will encourage him to lengthen his stride is your holding your whip arm out straight as you take longer steps.

At this point you should be lunging your horse at the walk

The sequence of footfalls at the walk.
  A. Right hind is down.
  B. Right fore is down.
  C. Left hind is down.
  D. Left fore is down. (*Photos by John Havey.*)

for no more than ten minutes at a time. Watch to see how he's reacting to what you're teaching him. If he doesn't understand what you want, you're just going to have to work a little longer on that particular exercise.

Most of any horse's fears and acts of disobedience are brought about by his owner or trainer and aren't the horse's fault at all. Always use your voice first. It's the aid your horse will understand best, and it's the one least subject to abuse. As your horse gets to know you better, you'll be surprised at how much a harsh, stern, disapproving tone of voice can change his attitude. Most people will punish a horse readily enough for misbehaving, but when the horse does something right they ignore it. They just continue to work him. How can the horse know whether he's done it right or not? And he has to know. Praise him with your voice and with good strong pats. You should always praise more often than you punish.

It's up to you whether you want the horse to come in to you or whether you want to go out to the horse at the end of the lesson. I prefer asking the horse to halt and then walking up to him. This way he knows that at no time do I want him to come in off the lunge line. Remove the side reins and the saddle and pat him. If you want, give him a tidbit, but I prefer telling a horse how great he's been rather than rewarding him with food, because in the future he'll look for food every time he's done something well.

If your horse is starting to sweat, cool him off, but he shouldn't be sweating very much. Overfed horses, or those on certain kinds of feed, tend to heat up easily, but the subject of feeding is beyond the scope of this book, and I suggest that you consult another authority about proper feeding.

Never end your training sessions when your horse is tired and misbehaving and your own temper is fraying. What will happen next is that you'll turn him out in his stall or pasture and not have anything more to do with him. Your horse is going to have the next 24 hours to think about what's just happened. If your training session ended on a sour, unpleasant note, he's going to remember it. If it ended on a positive note that was full of praise for him, he'll remember that. A willing horse learns faster than one that fears you and hates what he's doing.

5
The Trot

Urge your horse into the trot with your voice aid—a cluck or "trot" or whatever— at the same time that you push him forward with your whip. (You may have to use the whip a little more energetically than you had been using it.) If you use one aid without the other, your horse is likely to walk faster and faster until he's trotting. Don't let him rush off like that. Take him back to the walk and work on getting him to strike off from a nice, rhythmical, four-beat walk into a nice, rhythmical, two-beat trot. When he trots praise him.

Trot your horse until the circle that he's working on becomes very clear to him and he knows the **track** he's on. He may try all the tricks he did at the walk, pulling away from you or cutting corners. Help to relax him the same way that you did at the walk, remembering as you use the give-and-take motion with the lunge line that every stride of the trot has two beats, with a moment of **suspension** in between. You "give" with one beat (i.e., with every diagonal pair of legs) and you "take" with the next. By now you should be proficient enough to time these squeezing actions quite accurately and much more subtly than you were in the beginning—and from now on the word "hold" will be more appropriate than the word "take."

The trot is a steady gait with a very even rhythm, and it's a good gait for the horse to work at to learn balance and regularity of stride. But don't overdo it. Be sure to vary work at the trot with transitions to the walk and the halt, with

The horse isn't moving forward enough; his head has come up and his back is hollow. (*Photo by John Havey.*)

lengthening and shortening of stride, and with changes of direction—still by going up to the horse and walking him around. After each set of exercises, let your horse rest. He should have some time to relax and think about what he's just done.

You want your horse to be correctly on the bit in all his work on the lunge, even though the "bit" is still the lunge line connected to his cavesson. When he's on the bit, you'll feel in your hand the same light, elastic, even contact that you felt at the walk. The horse isn't pulling, but neither is the lunge line slack.

Remember that some horses, particularly those younger than four years old, will tire easily. If, after 10 or 20 minutes of hard work, your horse starts looking around and not

A good lengthening of stride, although the horse's frame could be slightly longer, with his nose slightly in front of the vertical. (*Photo by John Havey.*)

doing what you're asking him to do, and you know he understands what you want, you have to assume he's either bored or tired. Learn to recognize the signs of fatigue in your horse. If he starts looking unhappy and acting up on the lunge line—quit. But not immediately after he's done something wrong. First correct whatever he's done wrong, then continue working him on the lunge line for a minute or two more, doing something he does well. This is the way to finish all your training sessions. Let him do something he knows how to do and is good at. Finish on a positive, happy note.

If your horse is high-spirited, he may suddenly decide to act up or misbehave on the lunge. Say he's trotting and all of a sudden he starts to buck. Don't stop him. Don't ask for a halt; don't even ask for a walk, because to him this would be a reward—he doesn't have to work at the trot anymore. Make him keep right on trotting. Ignore what he's done and

A good working trot. The sequence of footfalls is:
A. Right fore and left hind are coming down. First beat.
B. Left fore and right hind are coming down. Second beat.
(*Photos by John Havey.*)

continue to keep him moving forward at the trot by using your voice and whip aids. Let him know you're not going to make anything out of this bucking silliness. It's very similar to dealing with the child who says a dirty word to his mother. If his mother interrupts what she's doing and turns around to him, even to chastise him, she's rewarded his behavior. He's gotten what he wanted out of her, which was attention. Things work very much the same way with a horse. If you simply ignore him when he acts up and continue working him at what *you* want him to do, you'll notice quite an improvement in his behavior.

The only time you should really chastise your horse is if he suddenly turns into the circle, or turns out, or stops. Reprimand him with a harsh, clipped tone of voice—"No!"—and mean "no." Then immediately put him back on the track that he was moving in and resume the trot. Don't let a couple of minutes go by before you reprimand him, because by then he won't know why he's being punished. You must react immediately after the horse has disobeyed, within seconds, and then continue working him. Once he's on the track again, praise him, using a light, affectionate tone of voice.

Some horses are downright lazy. If your horse wants to hang back, encourage him to trot forward first with your voice, and if that doesn't help, use your whip a little more vigorously. Move it along his side, lightly, from his flanks downward. Don't hit him with it, though, and if he moves on, praise him. If he doesn't move on, I'm going to qualify something I said earlier, and here is where you must be very honest in your understanding of your horse's temperament. If you know that his unwillingness to move forward isn't a result of anything except laziness, crack the whip behind you on the ground before bringing it to his hindquarters. At the same time, use your voice to reinforce the whip. You should only do this as a last resort, and you must understand that the whip is still being used only as an aid. You're not punishing your horse.

When you're working him, don't let him keep going in one direction, especially in the direction he seems to prefer. One of the things you'll have learned by this time from watching your horse is that he *has* a favorite direction. It's similar to right-handed and left-handed people, or the fact that most skiers find it easier to turn one way than the other. If your horse prefers going to the left, work him more going to the right (and vice versa), because he needs to get the muscles flexing properly on both sides of his body. If he doesn't like going to the right, it means he's a little stiff and uncoordinated on that side, and those are the muscles that need exercise.

At this point I want to introduce what's called the half-halt. Half-halts are an integral part of dressage and will be important to your horse throughout his training. A half-halt is a scarcely visible pause in the gait that encourages the horse to step farther under himself with his hindquarters. Although you can ask for a half-halt at any gait, either to prepare for a transition or to encourage engagement—I'll discuss their use at greater length in Part Four, Advanced Aids—I suggest that at first you ask your horse for half-halts only at the trot.

You achieve a half-halt from the trot by asking for the halt. Use your voice aid at the same time that you close your fist on the lunge line. Keep the whip moving slightly if your horse needs it. If he's high-spirited, don't use the whip at all, just your voice aid and your restraining hand on the lunge line. Just as your horse attempts to halt, *before* he has actually come down to a walk, ask him to trot on.

Now I want to backtrack for just an instant. If you have noticed during your work on the lunge line that your horse does not have a distinct, rhythmic, four-beat walk, he probably wasn't walking. He was ambling; his lateral legs (his left hind and left fore, for instance) were coming down simultaneously, or nearly so, instead of one at a time. If you cannot hear four distinct and perfectly rhythmic beats, ask your horse for a half-halt at the walk the same way you would at the trot. Just as he attempts to halt, ask him to walk on.

Remember not to keep working him at *any* gait for so long that he gets bored with it.

Once your horse is trotting easily and rhythmically and without resistance, introduce him to trotting poles. For the best results, you should have about four or five poles, each approximately seven feet long. Place them on the ground, parallel to one another, at four- to six-foot intervals, depending on the length of your horse's stride. For a 15-hand horse, try setting the poles approximately four feet apart. If your horse can adapt to a slightly longer stride, move the poles farther apart. First ask your horse to walk over the poles so he can look them over and smell them and see where they are. Then ask for the trot. Keep the horse on a large circle, and gradually begin moving in so that the horse has to come closer and closer to the poles and eventually has to trot over them.

Trotting poles provide good exercise for your horse because they'll help him bend the joints in his hind legs. You'll notice that he picks his legs up a little higher each time he goes over them. Since you can move the poles closer together or farther apart, they're also a good method for getting the horse to shorten or lengthen his stride—depending on how you place the poles. Make sure he maintains the same **tempo** and the same steady rhythm whether his strides have lengthened or shortened. The main thing is to watch that he doesn't rush over them or take steps between them.

Trotting poles are especially good for horses that tend to carry their heads too high, because all horses will stretch their necks down in order to see where the poles are.

Until now you've been working your horse for 15- or 20-minute periods. Gradually, over a month's time (and I give this loosely, because some horses learn faster than others), work up to half an hour, five days a week. Don't work your horse seven days a week; he should have a couple of days of complete rest. If you can't manage five days a week, at least be consistent; if you can only work your horse two days a week, it should be two days every week, not one day one week and four days the next. Horses fall into habits very quickly, and are happiest when everything in their lives runs according to routine.

It will probably take about a month until your horse is used to lunging, and by that I mean that he's accustomed to the lunge line and to going on the circle, and that he's used to your aids and feels relaxed and confident. Then you should be able to shorten the side reins one or two notches so the horse can seek a firm contact with them. Make sure both side reins are the same length, and that they're not so short that they bend his neck and pull his nose in. As you may have noticed, everything in dressage works from the hindquarters to the forehand, and the horse will bend properly, from the poll, with increased impulsion from his hindquarters. If you attempt to bend the horse's neck from the front, with side reins, he'll bend at the second, third, or fourth vertebra of his neck—a false bend—instead of at the poll.

Now is also the time to drop the stirrup irons so that the horse gets accustomed to the movement against his sides.

6
Engaging the Hindquarters

I've talked about the horse maintaining a constant, elastic contact with the lunge line, and explained that it meant he was on the bit. It also means that he's going forward with the correct rhythm and that he's relaxed and balanced. Now it's time to ask him to engage his hindquarters and begin using himself with some impulsion.

You ask your horse to engage his hindquarters by using your whip in a slightly different way. Sweep your whip forward on the ground towards his hindquarters, as usual. Then swing it up, as though you were tracing the upward slope of a hill, and let the lash fall of its own momentum by his hindquarters. (Some horses may need to feel the whip on their side or flank.) At the same time that you use your whip aid, use a supple give-and-take motion on the lunge line with your wrist. As your wrist "takes," use your whip to push the horse forward and use your voice aid slightly louder and stronger in the rhythm you want. As you "give," be sure to keep your wrist flexible, so that the horse can move into your hand *through* the lunge line without losing the contact. Don't drop the contact. Use one full stride to "take" and the next to "give."

Because the trot has a certain amount of natural speed, it's easier to ask your horse for engagement and impulsion while he's trotting. But as far as actually being able to see and understand what's going on, ask for it first at the walk. Start by watching your horse's hoofprints, especially the track that his inside legs leave: where he puts down his front leg and then where he puts down his hind leg on the same side. Now ask him to increase the length of his strides by using your voice and whip aids and your wrist on the lunge line in the manner I just described. Now watch the horse's footfalls again. The horse should be stepping *into* the hoofprint of his inside front leg with his inside hind leg, or even overstepping it. This is what engagement of the hindquarters means: the horse's stride has lengthened because he's stepping farther underneath himself with his hind legs. He's carrying more of his weight on his hindquarters, which lightens and raises his forehand. Once you see that the horse's hind foot is overstepping the hoofprint of the foreleg, immediately ask him to move into the trot. Keep asking him to trot forward with impulsion a few times around the circle. Then ask him to do something else.

Now that you know what it's supposed to look like, ask your horse for engagement and impulsion from the trot (and keep him at the trot; don't let him canter). If you're quick and you have 20/20 vision, you'll be able to see the same thing that you did at the walk: the horse is overstepping the hoofprints of his front legs with his hind legs.

Engagement is a visible change in the way the horse balances himself and carries his weight. Once he begins to stretch forward and lengthen his stride, his body will begin to bend along the curve of the circle he's on. This is called a **lateral bend.** It describes the increased flexibility of the horse's spine around the contours of a circle or a turn so that the horse is still able to move straight (i.e., the tracks of his hindquarters follow the tracks of his forehand). If you ask your horse for engagement too soon, he may resist you by throwing his hindquarters out from the track of the circle. (You can verify it by looking at his hoofprints. The tracks of his hind feet will be farther to the outside of the circle than the tracks of his front feet, forming a track of their own.) Since this is a very difficult fault to correct on the lunge line, take your time with the horse and don't rush him.

If you feel some slackness in the lunge line, it may mean that the horse isn't pushing his body forward into the rein—he isn't engaging his hindquarters. Use your whip then to encourage him to reach underneath himself with his hind legs. When he has engaged his hindquarters and is moving forward with impulsion, you'll feel the contact again.

If, instead of feeling slack, you feel him hauling on your hand, it's probably the same problem: the horse isn't engaging his hindquarters and is carrying most of his weight on his forehand. Encourage him with your voice and your lunge whip to move on at the same time that you give and take with a shorter, stronger action. This will keep him moving forward with rhythm, balance, and impulsion, but without speed. Another way to tell if your horse is carrying his weight on his forehand is to listen to the sound of his hoofbeats: the sound of his front feet striking the ground will be much louder than the sound of his back feet.

When your horse has found the correct contact on the lunge line, make sure he doesn't start leaning in on the circle. If you've ever ridden a bicycle, you know what it means to lean into a turn. Horses will do almost the same thing. You'll notice as the horse trots around on the circle that his inside shoulder and haunch are lower than his outside shoulder and haunch. What this means is that the horse is again leaning on his forehand. He's not reaching under himself with his inside hind leg, and as a result he's not moving forward into the bit. To correct him, ask him to move forward with equal impulsion from both hind legs by using your whip in the same way, in an upswept U, as you "hold" with the lunge line, but direct the whip toward his inside haunch so that he moves his hindquarters out. Move him forward into your hand and don't "give" to him. The

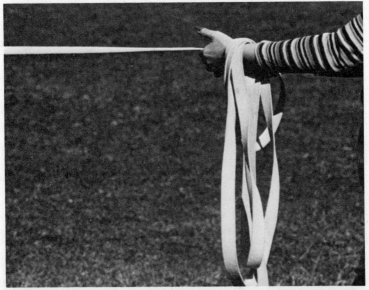

Funnel the lunge line through your hands like this to relax the horse. (*Photos by John Havey*.)

photograph on p. 139 in Chapter 13 shows a horse leaning in on the circle.

If your horse rushes off instead of engaging his hindquarters, try vibrating your lunge line, either in a small circle or back and forth, using your wrist in a slower than usual give-and-take motion. Horses generally calm down quite fast if you do this. Another way to calm a horse down is to let go of the whip (tuck it under your other arm, butt end frontward) and stroke the lunge line by funneling it back and forth through your hands as though you were reeling it in, speaking to the horse in a gentle, soothing voice.

Your horse should be moving forward calmly but energetically, and above all he should be attentive to you and to what you're asking him to do. Don't make the mistake of thinking that a horse that tosses its head and prances is being "energetic," or one that plods around and around with its ears flopping is "calm." The horse should be eager, not nervous, willing to move forward into your hands with long, unhurried strides and a relaxed, rounded back. Keep your horse awake and thinking "forward" by asking for a lot of transitions, changes of direction, half-halts, and so on. Eventually you'll be able to ask him to go from a halt immediately into a trot, but this requires a high degree of impulsion, so don't ask him to do it until you're sure he's ready.

Once your horse fully understands what's expected of him and has begun to use himself more energetically, you can ask him for a little more **collection.** You don't want anything radical, just a little more than the horse has been doing. (Every time you asked him to shorten his stride while maintaining the same rhythm and tempo, you were asking for collection.)

I prefer to ask for collection at the trot rather than the walk because when you ask a horse for collection at the walk there are a lot of other, less desirable things he can do instead. As you work with him, keep listening to his hoofbeats to make sure he maintains the one-two rhythm of the trot. If the rhythm changes—speeds up, slows down, or gets erratic—go back to the ordinary trot.

As the horse is trotting, encourage him to step even farther under himself with his hind legs and to lighten his forehand even more by sweeping the whip upward to his hindquarters and letting it fall, urging him on with your voice aid, and at the same time restraining him ever so lightly by closing your fingers on the line for one extra beat. You're asking the horse for more impulsion at the same time that you're telling him "Don't go faster."

In other words: you ask for collection by asking for increased impulsion with your voice and your whip while you simultaneously restrain with the lunge line. By "restrain" I mean that you don't "give." You contract your arm muscles just enough so that the horse can feel some resistance, and you hold that "don't give" for one beat longer than when you "do give."

It will help if you remember the triangle that your lunge line and your whip form with the horse. You're actually shortening the horse's frame between your lunge line and your whip by asking him to carry more of his weight on his hindquarters, which in turn lightens and elevates his forehand. This shortening of the horse's frame enables him to use himself with a little more energy, cadence, and brilliance. You want to collect that energy (a useful little pun; keep it in mind) and contain it in the horse. You don't want to let it out.

7
The Canter

At this point you can ask for the canter. The best and easiest way to ask your horse to strike off at the canter is to draw him into the circle a little. Shorten your lunge line just enough so that the horse turns into the circle a step or two with his forehand. As he starts to come in, ask for the canter with your voice aid. Then ask him to move out again and resume his circle by pointing your whip toward the girth. If you use the whip at the girth instead of forward from the hindquarters, it will prepare your horse for the leg aid when you ask for the canter from the saddle.

Increase the action of the whip if you have to, but don't make it look threatening. Some trainers bend down as they sweep the whip forward, then straighten as they bring the whip towards the girth, as if to let the motion of their body exaggerate the action of the whip.

By asking your horse to come into the circle with his forehand, you're giving more freedom to his inside foreleg. You always want him to lead with his inside foreleg in order to keep his balance. Watch your horse during his play time as he canters without the lunge line. The one foreleg that, with each stride, reaches higher than the other foreleg and lands in front of it is the one he's leading with. The correct leading leg at the canter is always the inside foreleg, and remember that inside means closest to the center of the circle.

Invariably, what your horse will do instead of canter is rush at the trot; in other words, shorten and quicken his strides and *then* break into a canter. Don't let him. Bring him back to a quiet, rhythmical trot and let him regain his confidence and his balance. Then ask him again. If he continues to rush off, make sure you bring him back down to a walk or trot every time. Talk to him. Quiet him down. Then ask for the canter again. Soon you'll find that he's relaxed enough to make the transition without rushing, and is cantering calmly and evenly. Praise him. Let him know he's done well.

Your horse isn't going to strike off into a canter if he's unbalanced. By now you should be able to tell immediately whether or not he's balanced. He must be going at the trot very obediently and rhythmically, bending laterally along the track of the circle, with his hindquarters well under him. Not until he's gotten to this point should you ask for the canter. If the tempo of the canter seems quite fast to you, you probably misjudged things and the horse didn't have his hindquarters balanced under his body sufficiently at the trot. When you asked for the strike-off into the canter he had most of his weight on his forehand. Be sure that he's bending his body in the direction he's moving in and that his hindquarters are engaged before you ask for the canter.

If your horse consistently strikes off on the wrong (**outside**) lead, nine times out of ten it's your fault, not his. You haven't been watching to see that he was bending correctly along the track of the circle. If his body is bending outward when you ask for the canter, with his head and neck and shoulders looking away from the circle, he'll invariably strike off on the wrong lead.

Another problem, especially with young horses, is that they'll strike off into a disunited canter. A disunited canter is one where the horse takes the correct lead with his hind legs, but doesn't follow through on the same lead with his front legs. If the horse were leading with his left foreleg, and if he were united, the stride would be: right hind, one beat; left hind and right fore, second beat; left fore the third and last

The horse is balanced and cantering on the correct lead. The sequence of footfalls is:

A. Right hind (one beat) is followed by left hind and right fore (second beat).

B. Left fore, the leading leg, is the third and final beat, followed by

C. A moment of suspension. (*Photos by John Havey.*)

beat; and then a moment of suspension. If he were disunited, he would be cantering with his left hind first, one beat; then right hind and right fore, second beat; then the left fore as the third beat. You may not be able to recognize that the horse is cantering disunited on the lunge other than that he seems to be unbalanced and the canter seems unusually rough or too fast. Correct him either by asking for a half-halt, using a short wrist action on the lunge line to further engage his hindquarters, or by asking him to come back to the trot. Keep him at the trot until he's regained his balance and is bending to the curve of the circle, and then ask for the canter again. Quite often a horse that's cantering disunited will correct himself by coming back down to a trot without being asked.

Instead of picking up a three-beat canter, some horses will pick up a four-beat canter. The extra beat comes in when the horse puts his hind leg down before he puts the diagonal foreleg down, instead of putting both down simultaneously. A four-beat canter means that the horse lacks impulsion, and you correct it by asking for a half-halt to help the horse engage his hindquarters. Frequent transitions will also help—trot to canter, canter to trot—and be careful not to stay at the canter for any length of time. Don't keep your horse at *any* gait for too long. He'll only get bored and tired and become unbalanced.

Striking off on the correct lead can be difficult for horses to learn. Don't give up on it, but don't lose your temper either and demand too much. If your horse isn't ready for it today, wait another day and try again.

It will help if you watch your horse during his play time. When you notice that he's about ready to canter, give him the voice aid you're going to use when you lunge him. If you can say this word to him a few times just as he breaks into a canter, he'll begin to associate the word with the action of cantering.

If your horse has a tendency to break back into a trot from the canter, let him. What this means is that he again has insufficient impulsion. Ask him for more impulsion at the trot, and continue asking for it once he's into the canter. You do this, once again, by watching him. Watch his hindquarters for the moment when both hind legs are on the ground. Then restrain him with your lunge line. Hold back, just a little, by closing your fingers quite firmly on the lunge line. Don't "give." At the same time, use your whip to encourage him to engage his hind legs under him more. This will lighten the forehand and add more weight to his hindquarters, which will give his canter more rhythm and cadence.

If your horse has difficulty slowing down from the canter to the trot (or from the trot to the walk), restrain him by using a longer holding action with your wrist on the lunge line. Don't haul on the lunge line, and be sure to use your voice aid.

Don't prolong your horse's work at the canter in the beginning. If he's cantering evenly, not too fast, and isn't pulling on the lunge line, once around the circle will be sufficient. You can gradually work up to more. Make sure that you've got all 20 feet of lunge line out so that the horse can canter on a fairly large circle. The smaller the circle, the more opportunties you're going to offer him to be unbalanced and rushed. If he rushes away at the canter or leans very heavily on his forehand, it may be because he's on too short a line and has to go on too small a circle.

When your horse is going evenly and rhythmically forward at the canter, you can ask for a little more collection. You ask for collection at the canter the same way that you did at the trot—by shortening the horse's frame between your whip and the lunge line. Ask the horse for more impulsion by sweeping the whip upward to his hindquarters and at the same time restraining his inclination to go faster by lightly closing your fingers on the lunge line for one extra beat. Restrain him after he has completed his stride; in other words, after the third beat, when the horse is suspended and before his outside hind leg touches the ground again.

Once around the circle at a collected canter is sufficient at this stage. Then immediately ask the horse to do something else. Although what he has done is by no means true collection, it is the *beginning* of collection the same way a lengthening of stride is the beginning of **extensions.** Always ask for a change of gait or a lengthening of stride after any type of collection.

Don't work your horse for more than half an hour, and don't wait until he's sweating profusely and looks exhausted before you quit. Finish before he gets tired. You don't want your horse to associate training with hard work. Conclude each lesson with something he does well and enjoys.

How much time you devote to training your horse on the lunge line will depend on his temperament, his conformation, and how well he understands what you're teaching him. I usually work horses on the lunge for at least two months, and sometimes for as long as a year. Dressage is a long road, and you have to have a lot of patience with it. And while two months might seem like an eternity, in the long run you'll agree that it was time well spent. When you begin to ride your horse, which is the next step, you're going to find it very easy, because you have done nearly all your work. Training your horse from the saddle will be much, much easier after you've put in the time lunging him.

Lunging is an art, and good lunging is very difficult to do. It's hard work that requires understanding of your ultimate goals and your particular horse's limitations. But you can accomplish a great deal through lunging. Athough I won't go into it here, I've seen horses trained by a style of lunging called "long reining" to Grand Prix level—Olympic level—without ever having had a rider on their backs.

8
Time Off and Trail Rides

After you've been lunging your horse for a couple of weeks, you're probably going to start feeling a little resentful. Here your horse is getting sleek and supple and mannerly, and all you're getting is eyestrain from trying to see where his feet land. You're itching to get on his back and go for a ride.

Go ahead. But please keep a few things in mind.

I've said I wasn't going to deal with young, unbroken horses. I'm assuming that the horse you've been schooling on the lunge has already been broken to ride. But some horses, especially in the West, are started as two-year-olds. In my opinion a two-year-old horse is too young to ride. The Spanish Riding School of Vienna doesn't allow its horses to be ridden until they're four, and the Lippizaners are big, stout horses that don't look as though they'd have a bit of trouble if they were started earlier. You *have* to wait until your horse is old enough to understand what you are teaching it and is physically capable of supporting your weight in the saddle. I don't allow my students to begin any work from the saddle until their horse is at least three, and that includes pleasure rides. If your horse is younger than three, lunge him to your heart's content, but even if he's already been broken, wait until he grows up before you ride him.

I encourage my students to alternate one day of training on the lunge with one day of pleasure or trail riding. Don't ride your horse the same day you work him on the lunge.

(But if your horse is at all high-spirited, do give him his play time first, and a few laps around the ring on the lunge line to get the kinks out.) I've stressed that you should end your training sessions before your horse gets tired, when he's still paying attention to you and doing well. If instead of ending his lesson and turning him loose, you saddle him up and go for a ride, you're telling him what he's just done wasn't good enough; if it had been good enough you would have rewarded him by stopping for the day.

Don't ride your horse the same place you lunge him; ride him someplace else, somewhere new and interesting. And don't cheat: if it's too cold (or too hot, or raining too hard) to lunge him, conditions aren't right for a ride. (If it is raining, I suggest you leave your saddle off when you lunge him.)

Those of you who live where the winters are mostly below freezing will probably have to give your horse the winter off, unless you have access to an indoor ring or you like riding in the snow wearing a face mask. Some people do.

Some people also like to ride bareback. I don't recommend it, even with a bareback pad. Your ultimate aim as a rider is to have a balanced seat, and it's next to impossible to ride a balanced seat bareback—you don't have a saddle to balance on. A saddle centralizes your spine and distributes your weight evenly over the horse's backbone. And even though you shouldn't depend on them, your stirrups will help your balance too—that's why they're there.

When you're ready to go out for the first ride, tack up your horse, using the same bit and bridle that you use for lunging. Leave off the side reins, and don't use any kind of martingale.

I said in the introduction that I was going to take you and your horse back to the beginning, and the only way to begin your ride is to get on your horse. Properly. The best explanation of mounting and dismounting that I know of is contained in *The Manual of Horsemanship of the British Horse*

Society and the Pony Club, published by Barron's Educational Series, Inc. of Woodbury, New York, a tremendously useful and informative little book that I recommend to all my students.

To mount your horse properly, first take up the reins in your right hand. Then slide your left hand down the reins until you feel contact with the horse's mouth. Your left hand should be on the horse's neck, a little above his withers. Take hold of some of his mane. Then turn so that you're almost facing the horse's hindquarters—actually you're facing the off-side hindquarter. With your right hand, turn your stirrup iron to face you. Slide your left foot into the stirrup iron all the way home, to the heel of your boot, with your toe pointing straight down. As you slide your foot in, put your right hand on the cantle and hop on your right foot (the one that's still on the ground) until you're facing across the horse's back.

If your horse is one of those that moves off when you're mounting, this is when he's going to do it: when you're half-way in the saddle and you have to hop along behind him on one foot. If you know he'll try to move forward, face him into the rail. Take up your reins a little—they probably have too much slack in them—and make sure they're even. If your horse still wants to move forward, use the same voice aid for the halt that you use on the lunge line, and "hold" him with your reins. Don't haul on them. When he halts, praise him.

If he tries to back up, slacken your reins—they may be too tight. If he keeps backing up, take your foot out of the stirrup and walk toward his hindquarters, still holding the reins. You are in effect *making* him back up, and he'll soon get tired of it and stop. Praise him. The only time you should get off the horse again while you're mounting is if he moves backward.

If he swings his hindquarters in toward you, take your

dressage whip in your right hand and very gently touch his hindquarters to keep him still. (When you ride with a whip, hold it in your left hand, with the reins, as you mount.)

If he swings his hindquarters away from you, it's probably because you're digging him in the side with your toe. Make sure that your toe is pointed straight down and away from his side.

If your horse hasn't moved at all, you're still standing with your left foot in the stirrup, facing across the horse's back, reins in your left hand and your right hand on the cantle. Now bend your right knee slightly, just enough to put you in a semi-crouch. This next part takes practice. What you want to do is push off with your right foot; you don't want to haul yourself up by your hands. Flex your knee slightly and then spring off the ball of your foot until both feet are the same height from the ground and your weight is supported by the stirrup iron. (You're still facing across the horse's back.) Move your right hand to the pommel of the saddle and swing your right leg over the horse's hindquarters. Do not graze his hindquarters with your boot—he might object.

Then, with some of your weight still on your hands, slowly and quietly settle yourself into the saddle. Don't plop yourself down like a sack of potatoes. Some horses will walk off as the rider's weight descends into the saddle. Other, so-called "cold-backed" horses, will hollow their backs in anticipation. These horses need to be mounted quietly, with the rider lowering his weight into the saddle slowly and carefully.

Once you've gotten your other foot in the stirrup, take up your reins, one in each hand. Close your fingers around the rein into a light fist, thumb uppermost, so that the rein passes from the horse's mouth through the funnel of your clenched hand—pinky, ring finger, middle finger, forefinger—and out between your thumb and forefinger. Some people hold the rein between their pinky and ring fingers. It depends on your hands. If you have strong hands, pass the rein between your pinky and fourth or ring finger. You can exert a surprising amount of leverage with your little finger.

When you're holding the reins properly, you should have very light contact with the horse's mouth. While the contact shouldn't be strong, the reins shouldn't be slack either.

If your horse still hasn't moved, give him a good pat on the neck and praise him with your voice. Then let him know you're ready to go.

As long as you're schooling your horse on the lunge line, don't worry about your position in the saddle. You're a passenger on your horse's back, literally just along for the ride. When you begin the next stage of training, from the saddle, you should sit properly all the time, even out on the trail. But until then, just try to relax as much as you can without falling all over the horse. Use your hands as little as possible and your legs not at all. No yanking, no kicking. Depend on your voice and a very light rein contact.

After you've been out for a while, and your horse has been walking along nicely and behaving himself, you're going to think "Why don't we try a little trot?" You can think it, but don't do it. Foresake your cowboy ways and *walk* your horse on the trail. Through lunging you've already put a lot of work into encouraging your horse to relax and trust you, and to move forward quietly and rhythmically. Until you understand what you should be doing to help your horse as a rider, don't risk exciting him and jarring his back or his mouth or knocking him off balance by trotting or cantering. You'll just undo weeks of training.

If your horse gets nervous about something on the trail, or if you think he's going to spook, talk to him. Stroke him on the neck, soothe him, let him know it's all right. But don't put him in situations where it isn't "all right." If you know he doesn't like water, don't take him through a bog. These rides should be relaxing for the horse as well as fun for you. Keep them as pleasant and uneventful as possible.

When you're finished with your ride, bring the horse to a halt and ask him to stand for a minute or two before you dismount. Don't prolong it, and when you sense the horse is getting fidgity, dismount before he decides to move.

Dismounting is almost the reverse of mounting. Pretend somebody took a movie of you while you were mounting. If they ran it backward, that's how you'd dismount. First, put your reins in your left hand. Then take your right foot out of the stirrup, place your right hand in front of you on the pommel, clear your right leg over the horse's hindquarters, and pause with your left foot in the stirrup, both legs straight, and side by side. Then—this part is a little different—place both hands on the seat of the saddle so that your weight is supported by your outstretched arms, and lock your elbows. The reins are still in your left hand. Kick your left foot out of the stirrup and jump down and away from the horse.

I don't recommend taking your right foot out of the stirrup, stepping down to the ground and standing there while you take your left foot out, which is the reverse of how you mounted. With one foot still in the stirrup you're in an awkward position, and if the horse shies, you're in trouble.

Pleasurable as trail riding can be, don't be tempted to stay out longer than half an hour. Like your training sessions, trail rides should be short and sweet, so that both you and your horse look forward to the next one.

Part Three
TRAINING FROM THE SADDLE– THE SADDLE– BASIC AIDS

9
An Independent Seat

Through lunging, your horse has learned to move forward rhythmically, with balance and impulsion. His confidence in you has grown noticeably, not only in his training but in his behavior in general. Now it's time for you to begin your own training as a dressage rider.

In the introduction I defined this stage of training as "straightforward riding." By that I mean you will concentrate on your own balance in obtaining an independent seat. As far as the horse is concerned, you will ride him straight, and you will ride him forward. From your work on the lunge you should have a pretty good idea of the basic meaning of "straight"—that the horse's hind feet are following the track of his front feet. "Forward" essentially means with a longer, more rhythmical stride. Your main concern as a rider will be with your seat, particularly your back and legs, and with using simple aids, most of them involving your balance, to ask the horse for transitions, engagement and impulsion, and increased flexibility of his joints.

While you're trying to master an independent seat, keep your lessons as short and interesting as possible. Make sure that your horse doesn't get bored. What is guaranteed to bore him faster than anything else is your practicing the same exercises over and over, in the same order, day after day. (People who are trying to learn the rising trot are notoriously single-minded.) Your horse will get resentful and start acting up, and you'll get mad and reprimand the horse, and it's all very pointless. Vary your lessons. Use as many transitions and changes of direction and tempo as you can. Then take the horse out in a pasture or on the trail and continue your riding there for a couple of days. When you work in the ring, play music. Music will help you keep the rhythm of the strides, and horses seem to like it too.

Until you've practiced enough so that you have a balanced seat, I advise you to use another horse. Your horse is already balanced—in effect, right now he knows more than you do. You're going to have to learn to sit correctly before you do anything else in dressage, and you're going to have to spend a lot of time on it. What's correct for one type of riding—jumping, or saddleseat, or Western—isn't correct for dressage. In dressage, your seat is independent of every other part of your body. You're in that saddle because you're balanced, not because you're gripping with your legs or holding onto the reins for support. Only through balance will you be able to feel the rhythm of the horse's hind legs and move with it, and learn how to use your aids to ask for more impulsion and refinement. At first you'll be doing a lot of bouncing and scrambling just to stay in the saddle, especially at the trot. Your horse is going to react by hollowing his back. This is contrary to everything you're working toward. The horse's back has to be rounded and relaxed in order for him to engage his hindquarters under him. By forcing him to hollow his back, you're undoing a great deal of what you accomplished on the lunge. And if your horse is at all high-spirited, he'll get excited. The more you bounce, the more uneven his gaits will become; he'll start going faster and faster and you'll spend most of your training session calming him down.

Using another horse is good practice for you too, since no two horses move identically and each has his own little foibles. But if another horse isn't available to you, you'll just have to use your own. Your best protection against jarring his back or exciting him is to know exactly what you should be doing *before* you get in the saddle.

So—let's get on with it. Your first step is to tack up your horse and lunge him for about 10 minutes. (But before you lunge him, let him have his play time.) After you've asked for the walk, the trot, and the canter in each direction, halt the horse and remove the cavesson, then reattach the side reins *beneath* the bridle reins.* Don't change the length. Before you mount, be sure to check the girth. Since you've been practicing the correct way to mount and dismount every time you've gone for a trail ride (*see* Chapter 8, if you'd like to refresh your memory), your horse will stand quietly and not move off until you tell him to.

While he's at the halt is the time for you to find your balance in the saddle. Your position will change somewhat as you progress to more advanced levels of training, but for what you'll be doing now this is what you should look like and how you should feel.

Your seat depends almost entirely on the correct placement of your seatbones in the saddle. Sometime when you're sitting in a chair, slip your hands under your buttocks. The sharp bones that you feel touching the seat of your chair are your seatbones. And the correct placement is as deep as possible into the lowest part of the saddle. Most riders sit too far back, which concentrates too much weight on the horse's loins. The first thing you should do is grip the pommel of the saddle with one hand and pull your seat toward your hands by tucking the base of your spine under you. You should feel your seatbones slide into the deepest part of the saddle. They should be in there so deeply and firmly that they won't slip out. Then stretch your body straight up, with your spine straight. You should be able to

* The photographs in this section were taken without side reins for the sake of clarity.

feel yourself literally balancing on the triangle formed by the end of your spine and the tips of your seatbones. The end of your spine should be exactly in the center of the saddle and your seatbones should lie on either side of that center point.

Your first tendency when you're trying to establish your seat will be to stiffen. If you stiffen, you'll pinch your buttocks together, and you don't want that; you want a wide base that you can balance on. Once you relax, your seatbones will open and spread, and you'll be able to feel yourself securely balanced on them in the deepest part of the saddle. If you stiffen your buttocks, you'll stiffen the rest of your body and communicate "stiffness" to the horse. To relax him, you have to be relaxed.

In general, if something hurts, it probably means that you're doing it wrong. The exception is your seatbones. After you've put in twenty minutes or so of hard work on the horse's back, your seatbones will hurt. You may find they hurt so much that you won't want to sit down. All I can say is, persevere. You'll get used to it.

When you're sitting correctly, your thighs should be turned in so that the big thigh muscle in the back of your leg lies flat and smooth against the saddle. You should be able to feel the horse's sides with the insides of your legs, from your thighs all the way down to your ankles, without having to squeeze. The easiest way to achieve this contact is to put your hand behind your thigh, about halfway between your knee and your buttock (the part you can get a good grip on), and turn the back of your leg out from under the bone. Rather than give my students lengthy instructions about how their thighs should be placed, I've found it's easiest to have them turn their thigh muscle by hand to "show their leg" where to go. This position won't feel either very comfortable or very natural at first, but eventually it will become second nature to you—whether the horse is walking, trotting, or cantering. You'll feel that your thighs and knees are

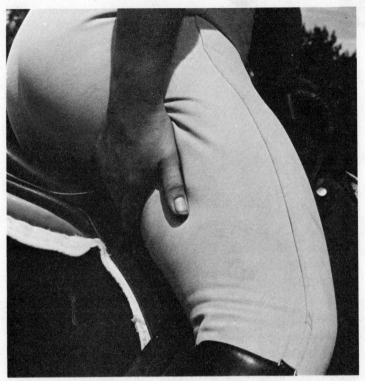

Turning your thigh out by hand. (*Photo by George Wrightson.*)

in such close contact with the saddle that you won't have to grip with your legs no matter what your horse does—no more lost stirrups and frantic scrambles to stay in the saddle. (If you clamp the horse's sides with your legs, you'll draw your knees up, and sooner or later you'll lose your stirrup irons.) The position of your thighs has as much to do with a balanced seat as the position of your seatbones, and flattening the insides of your thighs will also spread your seatbones. Practice settling your seatbones into the deepest part of the saddle and then turning your thighs out behind the bone (using your hand) every time that you get on your horse until the position feels natural to you.

The important thing to remember about an independent seat is that all the parts of your body are connected, like the old song about "the headbone connected to the neck bone." If the position of one part of your body is wrong, it's going to force the rest of your body out of alignment and ultimately affect the horse. If you're sitting wrong, you'll move wrong, and the horse will too.

With that old song in mind, let's go over the position of the rest of your body.

Raise your head. You should be looking straight ahead, over your horse's ears. Look toward the horizon. Get a fix on a tree, or the skyline—anything that will help you to keep your eyes on a plane parallel to the ground. And you should always, unless your horse is backing (and I won't deal with the rein-back in this book), look to the direction in which he's going.

Next, tuck your chin in. Pretend you're trying to show somebody how to make a double chin. Earlier, in the chapter on the rider's clothing, I suggested that you wear a shirt or blouse with a stiff collar. Now you know why: so that when you tuck your chin in, you can feel the shirt collar against the back of your neck. It's the only way you'll be able to tell at first whether your head and neck are straight. (If you have someone watching you from the ground, a stiff collar will also help him or her tell whether you're sitting straight.) Many people want to ride looking down at their horse's shoulder. The only times you should have to do this are to see whether you're rising on the outside diagonal or whether your horse has taken the correct canter lead—and both these things are far in the future. With these two exceptions, there is absolutely no reason you should be looking anywhere except straight ahead.

Next, think about your shoulders. Your shoulder blades should lie flat against your back. If you round your shoulders and try to hunch forward, your shoulder blades will stick out. If you're tense, you'll raise them—the way you would if you shrugged and said "I dunno." ("I dunno what I'm doing up here looking at trees and pretending I have a double chin.") Relax. I suggest to my students that they roll their shoulders around to the front, then roll them up and back. This movement will loosen up your shoulders, and when you feel that your shoulder blades are almost touching in back, you're sitting correctly. At first it will probably feel very erect and military to you. But if you practice the rolling exercise I just described, it will help you to loosen up and relax.

Your back (your spine, in other words) should be straight. If you round your back and shoulders, you'll add more weight to the horse's forehand and make it next to impossible for him to engage his hindquarters. Stretch your spine up without stiffening. The small of your back should be firm, so you can use it, but don't hollow your back. (I'll be dealing with the small of your back again when you begin using more advanced aids.) Your spine should always be flexible. You'll be able to follow your horse's movements only if your back muscles are supple, not rigidly clenched. Your entire upper body should be relaxed. But don't go to the opposite extreme and slouch, because you can't balance that way. A good way to "feel" the correct position of your back and shoulders is to stand with your shoulder blades and the base of your spine flat against a wall. Flatten as much of your spine against the wall as you can without hunching your shoulder blades. That erect, straight-up-and-down posture is the position you want in the saddle.

Your upper arms should hang almost straight down from shoulder to elbow. You should be able to feel the point of your elbow at your waistline. (This position will be familiar to you because this is how you lunged your horse.) Your upper arms should never move either ahead of or behind your body. If the person on the ground were to look at you sideways, in profile, he should see only the arm closest to him. Bend your arm at the elbow at approximately a 45-de-

Holding the reins correctly. (*Photo by George Wrightson.*)

gree angle, so that your entire lower arm, from elbow to wrist to knuckle, forms a straight line through the reins to the horse's mouth.

Your reins should be neither tight nor slack; you should be able to feel the same even, elastic contact that you felt on the lunge line.

The loop of the reins should fall on the right side of the horse's neck.

Check your arm and wrist position by glancing down—still keeping your head and neck straight—at your hands. All you should be able to see are your thumbnails, pointing towards the horse's ears, the knuckles of your index fingers, and (if you're holding the reins outside of your little finger)

Correct balanced seat. The rider's head and neck could be a little straighter. (*Photo by John Havey.*)

the nails of your two little fingers. (I discussed the correct way to hold the reins in the preceding chapter.)

There are several different schools of thought on the correct position of your hand and wrist. I teach my students to hold the reins so that their right thumb is pointing toward the horse's left ear, and their left thumb is pointing toward the horse's right ear. The wrist will be very slightly rounded, and most riders find it easier to relax their wrists in this position. If I tell my students "keep your wrists straight," they

The balanced seat viewed from behind. Notice that the rider's hips are square with the horse's hips. (*Photo by George Wrightson.*)

tend to tense their muscles so much that they can't flex with the movements of the horse.

I've used the word "vertical" several times to describe your position in the saddle. If your neck and back are erect, and your elbows are at your sides, you'll be "straight," i.e., vertical. By now you're probably wondering whether your legs, too, should be straight up and down. The answer is no, they shouldn't be. However, if the person on the ground were still watching you, he should be able to draw a vertical line from the top of your head straight down through your ear, your shoulder, your hipbone, and the back of your heel.

Your knees will be slightly in front of that vertical line, and your lower legs will descend at an angle from the point of your knee so that they're in contact with the horse's body without gripping. If you turn your knees in against the flap of the saddle, your lower legs will automatically be in the correct position, lightly embracing the horse's sides. Never cling to him with your calf muscles. If you're correctly balanced, your legs will be directly under your seat. Your feet will be parallel to the horse's side, and your weight will come down through the backs of your legs to your heels. The stirrup irons should be on the ball of your foot, and your heels should be lower than your toes. Don't try to force your heels down. They'll come down naturally if you think of your weight coming down the backs of your legs through your Achilles tendon to your heels. If you try to force your heels down by tensing your legs, your muscles will contract and you won't be able to embrace the horse's sides. Your feet should be approximately in the center of the stirrup iron, slightly closer to the inside.

If your thighs are in the correct position, your toes won't turn out, because if your thighs are flat against the saddle, your knees are in the correct position, and if your knees are turned into the saddle, your feet will be parallel to the horse's sides.

Some riders push their buttocks out behind them so that they're resting on their pelvic bone. This position is called "crotch riding," and it will force your hips too far in front of the vertical, which in turn will force your legs too far back for you to balance properly. If you try to ride with your knees too far back so that your legs are straight up and down, you'll find yourself crotch riding.

The other extreme is called the "chair seat," and describes what you look like if you push your legs toward the horse's shoulders. It's also referred to as "putting your feet on the dashboard," and you'll see Western riders and people who ride saddleseat in this position. These riders are sitting too

How not to—a crotch seat. In addition, the rider has bent her wrists, destroying the straight line between the bit and her elbows. (*Photo by John Fry.*)

far back in the saddle, with their shoulders and backs rounded. This position will force you to sit on the backs of your thighs rather than on your seatbones; your toes will turn out and you'll be riding on the backs of your legs rather than on the insides of your legs. If the position of your knees is too high, your legs will move forward, and you'll adopt a chair seat to balance yourself. A good way to check your position is to look at your boots when you've finished riding for the day. If there's dirt or a line of wear along the inside,

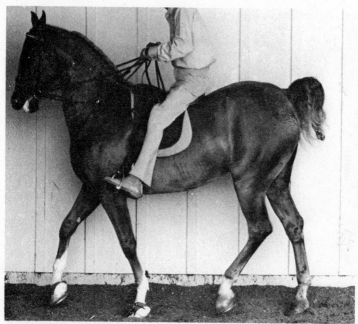

How not to—a chair seat. (*Photo by Joan Fry.*)

you were sitting properly. If they're dirty on the backs of your calves, you were sitting in a chair seat.

Often you can see daylight between a rider's knees and his saddle. What this should indicate to you is that his thighs aren't in the correct position, which has forced his knees out and away from the saddle and pushed his feet out at right angles to the horse's sides.

Once you've found the correct position, you may find that you'll have to adjust your stirrups. If you've been taught to measure the length of your stirrups against the length of your arm, they'll probably be too long. Adjust the leathers so that you can slide your boot easily into the stirrup iron as you're sitting correctly in the saddle. You shouldn't have to

The balanced seat from the rider's point of view. The rider's feet appear to be too far off the horse's sides, but this is an optical distortion caused by the camera lens. (*Photo by George Wrightson.*)

change the position of your knee at all, either to raise your leg or lower it, in order to find the stirrup iron. Adjust the stirrups to the correct position of your legs; don't adjust your legs to the stirrups.

Achieving a balanced seat and maintaining it without changing your position through the various gaits and exercises will require a considerable amount of practice. Think about your position in the saddle constantly: can you feel yourself balanced on your seatbones? Are your thighs flat against the saddle? Is the back of your neck touching your shirt collar? Are your shoulder blades flat? How much of your hands can you see?

Another check you can run on yourself is to glance down at your knees from time to time, still keeping your neck and head in the proper position. If you're sitting correctly, you should be able to just barely see the rim of your boot toe. If you can see the entire toe, you're either hunching over the pommel or your legs are too far forward. If you don't see any toe at all, either you're too far back or your legs are too far back. Your upper body should be balanced on your seatbones, your lower legs should be gently embracing the horse's sides, and you should be *relaxed.*

10
The Walk

Your horse, patient animal, is still standing quietly at a halt, waiting for you to figure out how you want to sit on him. Once you're assured that you're sitting with a balanced seat, ask him to walk on. Remember that you only have a light contact with his mouth. The reins aren't tight, but there's no slack in them either. Ask him to walk on by leaving your hands exactly where they are and squeezing with both your legs. Your legs should be touching him at the girth; close your leg muscles in short nudges so that the horse can feel a slight pressure against his sides. He will respond by walking on. When he does, release the pressure of your legs and stroke his neck in long, firm strokes, one hand at a time, still holding onto the reins. By praising him in this manner you're getting him used to the bit moving in his mouth and showing him that it doesn't hurt.

If he doesn't move off, aid with your dressage whip. (And here's another way for you to check your position in the saddle. You're holding your dressage whip—and I hope you have one—in your inside hand, so that the top is about an inch from your thumb and index fingers. If your arm and hand aren't in the correct position, the whip won't touch the horse's side unless you move your wrist.) If you've asked him once with your legs and he hasn't moved off, ask him again. As you close your legs, very gently touch him with the whip. If he still doesn't move off, try again. Not harder, though. Use the whip at the same time that you squeeze with

The correct way to hold a dressage whip. (*Photo by George Wrightson.*)

your legs. You must never use the dressage whip alone. It has replaced your lunge whip, and you use it to reinforce your legs the same way you used your lunge whip to reinforce your voice aid.

It may take a couple of tries, but sooner or later your horse will move off. Reward him extravagantly, using your voice and pats on his neck. Let him know he did exactly what you wanted him to do.

For the first five minutes or so let him walk around the ring without trying to turn him or influence where he goes. He'll probably either follow the fence line or go in big circles, since he's used to that from the lunge line. As he walks, let your body follow his movements. Don't stiffen up, and especially don't pinch your buttocks together. Concentrate

Stroking the horse's neck to relax him. (*Photo by George Wrightson.*)

on letting your back move with the movements of his back. If you're relaxed, you'll feel them.

Both your seat and your back should be moving back and forth to the rhythm of the horse's walk. Don't try to exaggerate this motion or set up a rhythm of your own; let the horse move you. Relax and follow the movements of his back.

Your hands should still maintain an even contact with the reins, but this doesn't mean your hands move back and forth with the movements of the horse's head and neck. Hold the reins in a light, even contact, and hold your arms still.

By the end of five or ten minutes you should feel confident of keeping your seat at the walk. You've checked the position of your neck, shoulders, hands, and boots, and you think you're balancing correctly on your seatbones. Now I want you to try a few very simple exercises. They will help you maintain the correct rhythm of the walk, and they will help you gain confidence in your seat. They will also prepare you for subsequent work at the trot.

First, slide your hand up the reins, still keeping the same light, even contact, and tie a knot in them. Now drop them on the horse's neck. Because there's a knot in them, you won't lose them if your horse decides to do something funny. (And if your horse is on the excitable side, do this exercise very quietly, with as little fuss as possible. Soothe him with your voice so that he knows there's nothing much going on, and certainly nothing that's going to harm him.) Then, grasp your dressage whip in front of you with both hands so that the whip is parallel to the ground and there's a space about as wide as your hips between your two hands, and raise your hands straight up over your head. Your arms should be far enough behind your head so that you can't slump forward without moving your arms too. As your horse walks, you stretch. Stretch your stomach and back as though you were trying to push a cloud up with your whip. Try to feel the stretch in your stomach muscles. In this position, concentrate on the horse's movements again. You'll find that you can feel the influence of the horse's back very strongly, and you'll find your body moving with the rhythm of the horse's body.

Simple as it is, this is an invaluable exercise, and one I recommend to advanced riders as well as beginners. With practice, you'll become confident enough in your balance to do this exercise at the trot and canter. Since it's especially good for achieving and maintaining a balanced seat, even very experienced riders will go back and practice it. It will help you realize that it's your seat that's keeping you in the saddle, not the reins or your legs.

Here's another exercise which will give you confidence in your seat. Untie your reins and take them up in your inside hand. With your outside hand, take hold of the pommel and straighten your arm so that you're pulling your shoulders back and pulling your seat toward your hand at the same time. This is the same thing you did when you first mounted to pull yourself forward into the deepest part of the saddle. Stay in this position for a couple of minutes as the horse walks around, and try to feel with your seatbones that you're deep into the saddle. Remember to keep your legs in the correct position. As you begin working on the trot and canter, there will be times when you're not in contact with the horse—in fact, not even in contact with the saddle. Rather than bouncing helplessly and jarring your horse's back, you can literally pull yourself into the saddle by grasping the pommel. Practice now, at the walk.

Another even simpler exercise is to cross your stirrups in front of you over the horse's withers. Ride, at the walk, without stirrups, keeping your thighs, knees, heels, and toes in the correct position. Don't relax and turn into jelly just because you don't have your feet in the stirrup irons. Hold your toes up and feel the weight coming down into your heels. This exercise will also help you to feel the back-and-forth motion of the horse's back in your seat, and enable you to move with it.

In Part Four I'll describe more advanced aids for the walk, as well as for the other gaits, but for the time being the emphasis is on you, the rider, and your balance, coordination, and rhythm in the saddle. You know what the correct rhythm at the walk should be from watching your horse on the lunge line and feeling it in your seat through the exercises I've just described. The walk should always be rhythmical, brisk without being fast, and energetic. Your horse must never just slouch along dragging his feet, even out on the trail.

As your horse is walking, watch his shoulders. You'll notice that they rotate: the right shoulder moves up, forward, down, back, and up again. The left shoulder does the same thing. As the right shoulder moves up, apply a light pressure with your *left* leg at the girth. As the left shoulder moves up, squeeze with your *right* leg. At the walk use your legs alternately, not both legs at the same time. What you ultimately want to do is influence the movement of the horse's hind legs. Remember that the sequence of footfalls at the walk is right front, left hind, left front, right hind, with three feet on the ground at all times. Concentrate on feeling the horse's hindquarters move under you through your seat. Soon you'll be able to feel that what happens after the left shoulder moves up, forward, and down is that the right hind leg moves up, forward, and down. By influencing him with your leg as his shoulder moves up, you're actually influencing the step he's about to take with the diagonal hind leg, and regulating and refining his rhythm.

If your horse mistakes what you want and starts to go faster, ask him to slow down, but not—at this point—with your hands or back. Use your voice. Use the voice aid you did on the lunge line, "easy," or whatever, and the rhythm of your body. Stop letting your body move with the horse. Slow down your own rhythm as you use your voice aid so that the easiest thing for the horse to do is slow down too.

By now your horse has probably been going around and around the ring in one direction for quite some time. Unless you ask for a change of direction, he's going to get bored and very stiff on one side. Ask him for a **change of rein** (a change of direction) by cutting across the long side of the ring on the diagonal. The usual riding ring has two long sides and two short sides. Say you've been going to the right, on the right rein. Turn a horse's length past the second short corner by asking the horse with one aid only: your inside (right) rein. Keeping your upper arm in the normal position, move your right hand and lower arm out and away from your body. By doing this, you're opening and flattening the right side of the bit in the horse's mouth. (The bit normally lies in a V position.) Continue across the long side of the ring

Opening the inside rein to change direction. (*Photo by George Wrightson.*)

on the diagonal. When your horse reaches the rail, he'll be going in the opposite direction, to the left. If your horse responds very quickly to this open rein, gradually decrease the angle until you're barely opening your arm. Eventually you'll be able to turn him simply by applying a little more pressure on the rein with your little finger, but—since this involves other, more advanced aids—work from the open arm position for the time being and make sure that your turns are quite large.

When you ask your horse to turn, you shouldn't be influencing him in any way—either with the opposite rein or your legs. But if you feel a little tension in the opposite rein as the horse turns, allow your arm to slip forward a little. Don't let the rein slide through your fingers.

Riding circles is another good exercise, since they will get the horse accustomed to working away from the rail. Ask for a circle the same way you ask the horse to change direction, by opening your inside rein. Make sure that your circles are still quite large, no smaller than approximately 40 feet in diameter, and try to make them round. Try to keep the angle of your arm the same all the way around the circle. This will keep the horse's head and neck bent at more or less the same degree and will help him to make round circles without drifting.

As your horse is walking, try some other exercises. They only take a few minutes to do and they're well worth the effort in the additional confidence they'll give you in your seat.

First, rotate your head around on your neck, rolling it as far forward and to the side and back as you can without moving any other part of your body. (As in all the exercises, the parts of your body not being exercised must stay in the correct balanced position without moving.)

Then knot the reins on your horse's neck, stretch your upper body, and raise your arms to shoulder height, straight out. Rotate both arms from the shoulder socket in small circles, first in one direction then in the other. Gradually enlarge the circles, then decrease them.

Next, raise both arms up over your head. Bring your right arm forward over your horse's left shoulder and try to touch your left toe. Your seat *must* stay in position in the saddle. Straighten and then try to touch your right toe with your left hand. Repeat the exercise 10 times with each arm.

Raise both arms straight over your head again. Bending from your hips, lean forward over the horse's neck and try to touch his poll with your hands. It's important that you bend from the hips and that you not lose contact with the saddle with your seat. Straighten, then lean straight back, so that your back is flat on your horse's rump. Some horses are skittish about being touched on the hindquarters, and if yours is one of them, don't do the second half of the exercise just yet. The first few times you try it, ask someone to hold the horse, and do it at the halt.

After each exercise, be sure to pat the horse and let him know that everything's fine. He might be getting a little nervous about all these strange goings-on.

Next, put both hands on your hips and rotate your body from the hips as far as you can without moving your seat, first one way, then the other.

The number one problem beginning riders have is a tendency to curl their seat under them, which results in a rounded back. In the following exercise try to keep your seatbones in a normal position in the saddle. First, put your hands on your hips and take your feet out of the stirrup irons. Then raise your knees up toward your chest as high as you can. The trick to this exercise is that your entire leg, from the inside of your thigh all the way down to your heel, should not touch any part of the horse or the saddle. In other words, you have to spread your legs apart a little in order to draw your knees up, and to allow your back and seat to move with the horse. This exercise is very beneficial in helping you to move in rhythm with the horse, and is especially helpful for identifying the sequence of footfalls. When you absolutely can't hold your knees up any longer, lower your legs so that they're in the correct riding position, only don't put your feet in the stirrup irons. Instead, swing your lower legs alternately back and forth along the horse's sides. Do this about 10 times.

When you've mastered this exercise at the walk, try it at the trot—after you've mastered sitting to the trot. But don't attempt it unless you have confidence in yourself, your seat, and your horse.

Here's another one: with your feet out of the stirrup irons, rotate your ankles first in one direction, then in the other. This exercise will loosen your ankle joints and make it easier for you to keep your feet in the correct position.

To stretch your thigh muscles and help them to lie flat against the saddle, grasp your right toe with your right hand and draw your foot up and out behind your seat as far as

The bent knee exercise. (*Photo by John Fry.*)

you can. Then lower your foot back into the stirrup iron, making sure that your upper leg, from the knee up, remains in the stretched position. Then do the same with the other leg. This exercise will give a longer line to your upper leg; when you stretch your leg out behind your seat you're really stretching the knee *down,* and you'll be able to feel the pull in your thighs.

These exercises will make you more supple and will also give you more confidence. After you've done them and have taken the reins back and are stitting correctly, you'll feel much looser and a lot more relaxed. In consequence, you'll have a better seat.

When you've put in 20 minutes or so of practice the first day, quit. (I don't recommend that you ever spend more than half an hour at a time working on your seat.) This means you have to bring your horse down to a halt. The only aid I want you to use in downward transitions at this stage is your voice. Use the same voice aid that you did on the lunge line. In fact, this will tell you how much your horse has learned on the lunge. Tell him "halt," or "HO-ho," or whatever you've been using. If the horse doesn't respond, simply hold your hands very still without any kind of a "giving" motion at all. Nothing more. You will *never,* from this day forward, pull back on the reins. In dressage you want the horse to move forward with his hindquarters under him, and if you lean back, or pull back on the reins, you'll upset his balance and defeat your own purpose. At this point you must rely on your voice and patience for all things.

When the horse halts, stroke his neck and ask him to stand quietly for a minute or two before you dismount. If you've been taking him out on the trail, he already knows how to do this; now increase the time a little. He should stand absolutely still with his weight equally balanced on all four legs. At first, you'll probably have to twist around and look down at his feet to see whether he's standing square. If he's not, if his right hind leg is behind his left one, for instance, touch *your* right leg against his side very slightly so

The halt. (*Photo by John Havey.*)

that he moves his leg up. If he doesn't respond, touch him lightly with the whip. When he has moved up and is standing square, praise him. Eventually you should be able to feel whether he's standing square or not, and to correct him without looking down.

The instant you sense he's getting ready to shift his weight, praise him and dismount. During subsequent training sessions practice a lot of mounting, halts, and dismounting. Nothing is worse than a horse that fidgets and walks off as you're trying to mount or dismount. Practice until your horse is sure of what you want and can do it willingly and without confusion every time you ask him.

11
The Rising Trot

In many respects the trot is the best gait at which to train a horse and correct his mistakes. Since his weight is carried evenly on all four legs (in comparison with the walk or the canter), it's the best gait to use to teach him regularity and rhythm. Unfortunately for the beginner, the trot is also the worst, bounciest, most bone-punishing gait the horse has evolved. For all these reasons, you must learn how to ride the trot correctly, now, before you do anything else.

There are two acceptable ways a rider can deal with the trot. One is to post; the other is to sit to it. (I'll deal with the sitting trot in the following chapter.) You should learn the rising or posting trot first, simply because it's easier on the horse, and—although you won't believe this at first—on you. Your balance still isn't what it should be, and while you're trying to move with the horse's rhythm at the trot, it's easier on his back if you're out of the saddle part of the time.

To get your horse from the walk into the trot, use the same voice aid that you did on the lunge line. If he trots, praise him. If he doesn't, influence him with your legs by using the same short squeezes that you did to get him to move off into a walk. As you ask with your voice aid, close your legs gently against the girth by contracting your calf muscles and nudging with your ankles. It's highly unlikely that any horse, no matter how lazy, won't trot off. But if he still doesn't understand, or prefers to keep walking, influence him with your whip. Use your voice and touch the

The three phases of the posting trot. First, the rider allows the horse to push her out of the saddle. (*Photo by John Havey.*)

horse's side with the whip directly behind your heel at the same time that you apply pressure with your legs in short, energetic nudges.

Now that your horse is trotting, what are you doing? In theory, there are four main things to concentrate on as you're doing the rising trot. The first is to let the movement of the horse push you up out of the saddle; the second, to pull your hips forward toward your hands as you go up; the third, to keep your shoulders back; and the fourth, to keep your weight in your heels. In practice, you're going to feel as though a lot of things are happening at once, and it's going to be very difficult for you to separate them into categories

Then she thrusts her hips forward into her hands. (*Photo by John Havey.*)

as you're bouncing all over the saddle. I encourage my students to concentrate on one thing at a time. If you have memorized this short list of things to concentrate on before asking your horse for the trot, your work will be considerably easier. And if you ride to music, often the rhythm of the music will help you with your own rhythm.

First, let the movement of the horse push you forward. The trot, as you know, is a diagonal gait with two beats. You rise out of the saddle on one beat and come back down on the other. Count the beats "one-two, one-two," and then substitute "up-down, up-down," in the same rhythm. As you become more aware of the horse's rhythm, it won't take any effort at all on your part to push forward on the "up" count.

When the horse's outside foreleg and diagonal hind leg are on the ground, she sits down in the saddle. (*Photo by John Havey.*)

The horse will do it for you. Don't try to lift yourself out of the saddle by using your stirrup irons. And don't try to push off by straightening your knees when you come out of the saddle and bending them when you come back down. The rising trot is not performed from either your knees or your stirrup iron. It is performed from your seat, through your hips and thighs.

Once you begin to feel the horse's rhythm pushing you out of the saddle, pull your hips forward toward your hands as you go up. Lean forward from your hips, not your waist, and roll forward onto your thighs. You're not gripping with your thighs, but if they are in the correct position, you

Here the rider is leaning forward and using her stirrup irons to push off from. (*Photo by John Havey.*)

should be able to roll forward on them as you rise out of the saddle and roll back on them as you sit down. It is essentially your thighs that absorb the jolting movements of the trot, and the motion you should work for is a back-and-forth motion with only a very slight up-and-down motion. When you've rolled forward into the front of your thighs on the "up" as far as you think you're going to go, push your hips forward into your hands. Don't jerk your body forward. Do it as smoothly as you can; it's a transition to get you back into the saddle without jarring the horse's back.

When you roll back on your thighs and come "down" into the saddle, don't push your seat behind you. If you have pushed your hips toward your hands when you were "up," your seat will be neatly and properly tucked under you, with your seatbones coming into the deepest part of the saddle. If you come down with your seat out behind you, you haven't tucked your hips in enough. You were probably leaning too far forward and hollowing your back. You should come down in the correct, balanced seat position, with your seatbone directly under your shoulders.

The next thing to concentrate on is keeping your shoulders back. As you rise forward into your thighs, lean slightly forward from your hips, with your neck, back, and shoulders in a straight line. Be sure that your shoulder blades are flush with your back and that your back isn't rounded or hollow. (Also be sure that your arms remain in the correct position, and that you don't raise them as you're going "up.") Most beginning riders try to lean too far forward. I tell my students that there's a string attached to the top of their heads and that somebody straight above them is pulling it up and down, up and down. Then they usually get it right. If you roll forward with your shoulders straight and the muscles of your chest and stomach flexing upward, your back will be straight and you'll get the correct forward "tilt."

Your movements out of the saddle at the rising trot will actually be very slight, in spite of what it feels like. If you watch a good dressage rider doing the rising trot, he or she will barely seem to be moving. But in the beginning, don't worry about how much or how little you move. In fact, in the beginning, the most important thing for you to feel is that it's the *horse* that's pushing you forward into your thighs, and not anything that you're doing.

The fourth and final thing to concentrate on is keeping your weight in your heels. One of the reasons a very good rider will hardly seem to be moving at the rising trot is because his legs remain in the same position along the girth line all the time, whether he's going "up" or coming "down." Even though you bend forward into your thighs when you go "up," you must bend from your hips. Your legs don't move at all—and you should not be using your stirrups to push off from. If you try to push off from your stirrup irons, you'll push your toes down. But if you let the horse's movements push you forward into your thighs, your heels will stay down. (It will help if you remember to keep the stirrup irons on the ball of your foot.)

Your horse may get a little excited from all this activity on his back. But if he has learned balance and a steady rhythm from the lunge, he should be willing to maintain it from the confidence he has in you. But if you notice that he's trotting faster and faster, talk to him. Soothe him with your voice, and as you're posting, stroke his neck, one hand at a time, still holding the reins. If this doesn't help, keep the same length of rein, but hold the reins more firmly and don't "give"—the way you did in similar situations on the lunge line. Hold the reins still, but don't haul on them. Also remember that your elbows should never stick out behind you. It may take you a good 10 or 15 minutes to settle your horse down, but you must do it before you move on to anything else. He must have confidence in you, and in what you're doing, at all times.

When you have circled the ring a few times, concentrating on each of the four main points in turn, sit down in the saddle without rising to the trot. Don't go "up"—relax. Using your voice aid and holding the reins, ask your horse for the walk. Always sit down in the saddle for all transitions. When your horse comes down to a walk, praise him. Then let him walk around for a few minutes on a **long rein** while you both take a little break. At the end of any work period, or at the end of the lesson, always let the horse walk on a long rein so he can take a breather and think about what he's just done.

The next time you ask him to trot you're going to be rising on the outside diagonal. From your work on the lunge line you know that each "one-two" beat of the trot involves one foreleg and the diagonal hind leg rising and coming down together, and then the opposite foreleg and the diagonal hind rising and coming down. If you rise on the outside diagonal, it means that you're rising out of the saddle as the horse raises his outside foreleg and his inside hind leg. If you're going around the ring to the right, you'll be rising in unison with the horse's *left* foreleg.

Here's how you do it. When your horse starts trotting, the best thing to do is sit down in the saddle for a few strides and watch his outside shoulder. When it moves upward, count "up" and roll forward into your thighs and begin rising with the trot.

Get into the habit of rising on the outside diagonal every time you do a posting trot, because it will be a great help to your horse. If you're going to the right and rising on the left diagonal, you're coming out of the saddle as the horse's inside hind leg and outside foreleg move up, and you're coming down into the saddle as the horse's inside hind leg and outside foreleg come down. If you were to rise on the incorrect (in this case, the right) diagonal, your weight would be coming into the saddle just as the horse was trying to raise his inside hind leg. It would be more of an effort for him to raise that leg, and consequently he wouldn't raise it as high, or be able to reach as far under his body with it, as he would if you were on the correct outside diagonal. As you move into advanced training and begin asking for additional impulsion from your horse, you'll understand why it's so important for your weight to be out of the saddle as the horse raises his inside hind leg.

If you find yourself rising on the wrong diagonal, sit down for one extra beat and then start posting again. You should still be counting, "up-down, up-down." To change diagonals, count "up-down, *down,* up-down," and sit through the *down.* When you go "up" again you'll be on the correct diagonal.

When you ask your horse to change rein by going diagonally across the ring, you must change your posting diagonal to the new outside leg as soon as you ask him to turn at the second short corner. Make the transition the same way you would if you found yourself on the wrong diagonal, by sitting down for one extra beat. Make sure that your turns are still quite large, and that you ask for them by opening your rein in the direction you want the horse to turn.

Change directions frequently and practice transitions from the trot to the walk to the halt. Keep your horse at the halt for two or three minutes and then go back to the walk and then into the trot again. Don't ask your horse to go from a halt directly into a trot at this point.

By this time your thigh muscles are probably hurting. Don't be discouraged; the more you practice, the sooner they'll stop hurting. It will, I admit, take a lot of practice before you master the rising trot. It takes some riders as long as a month of daily work to get it right, but people learn things at different rates of speed, just as horses do, and it might not take you nearly that long. Do not have someone who has learned how to do a rising trot by using entirely different methods (such as someone who rides hunt seat) watch and correct you, because a rising trot in dressage isn't the same. It will help if you could prop a big mirror up against the rail and watch yourself, or talk a friend into taking some film of you with a movie camera.

But the best way to make sure you're doing the rising trot correctly is to test yourself. Since a lot of beginning riders try to push off from their stirrups, the first test is to take your feet out of the stirrup irons and do the rising trot without them. Roll forward into your thighs to rise, and roll to the back of your thighs to come down, the same way you did when you had stirrups. If you can still do it—and you're not gripping with your knees—then you're doing it correctly. A correct rising trot is about halfway between what you think it is when you're actually depending too much on your stirrups, and what you do without any stirrups at all. You can also test yourself to see whether you're depending on the reins (and thus your horse's mouth) to pull yourself out of the saddle. Put your feet back in the stirrup irons and tie a knot in the reins. As your horse trots, put your hands on your hips and do the rising trot. If, instead of putting your hands on your hips, you hold your arms and hands in the correct position, but without holding the reins, you can see whether you tend to let your arms float as you do the rising trot. Riding without stirrups at both the trot and the canter is one of the best methods that I know to help you achieve an independent seat.

Another exercise that will help your balance is what's called the "two-point position." The name refers to the position of your two legs when you're "up" at the rising trot. The difference between the two-point position and the rising trot is that in the two-point position you stay "up." You don't come "down."

Try it first at the walk. Rise forward out of the saddle into the front of your thighs in the "up" position, making sure that your seat is completely out of the saddle and tucked correctly under you, not stuck out behind you. Your legs should be in the correct position along the girth with your weight in your heels. Don't stand straight up in the stirrups and don't crouch over your horse's neck. You must be very relaxed. If you're tense, you won't balance. Stay in this "up" position, balanced on your thighs, without coming "down." Notice your balance and how your weight is distributed. If you're balanced, you'll have the definite sensation that your heels are sinking, as though your weight is falling through the backs of your legs into your heels.

Now ask your horse for the trot, but instead of posting, stay in the "up" two-point position. See if you can hold it for five minutes without stiffening or toppling over and without trying to grip. If you find yourself falling back into the saddle or falling over the horse's neck, you're either leaning too far back and are getting left behind, or you're too far forward. In either case, you're not correctly balanced. After you've held the two-point position for five minutes, start your regular rising trot again. And every time that you rise "up" out of the saddle, think of how your body felt in the two-point position.

Try the two-point position with a knot tied in the reins and your hands on your hips. If you want, hold the reins with one hand and a piece of mane with the other, but you'll be better off with your hands on your hips so you're not interfering with the horse's mouth.

A good exercise is to alternate trotting in the two-point position for 10 strides and then rising to the trot for 10 strides. Then change rein by turning up the diagonal—and remember to change your posting diagonal.

By this time you should feel confident enough to try the rising trot over trotting poles placed about 4½ to 5 feet apart. The only thing that will happen is that the horse will pick his feet up a little higher than he usually does and will want to lengthen his neck to look down at the poles. Let him—but don't let him pull the reins out of your hands. Instead, let your arms move forward with the horse's movements. Don't allow the horse to fall back into a walk, or try to hurry, or break into a canter. He must maintain a steady, even rhythm. Trotting poles are especially good for teaching a horse rhythm and cadence at the trot—hence their name. And make sure that you're still looking between your horse's ears, not down at the poles.

Once you've mastered the rising trot, you'll want to steady your horse's rhythm and ask for more engagement by aiding with your legs the same way you did at the walk. But instead of using first your left leg and then your right, use both legs together. Every time you're "down" in the saddle, aid by squeezing both legs gently against your horse's sides at the girth.

Soon you should be able to feel what diagonal the horse is on without looking. It will take time and a lot of trial and

The two-point position over cavaletti. (*Photo by George Wrightson.*)

error, but you'll be a better rider for it. If you ever ride a dressage test, you shouldn't look down. The first few times, rise to the trot without looking at your diagonal, and concentrate on feeling the movement in your legs and thighs. Then look down and check yourself. If you're on the wrong diagonal, sit down for one beat and concentrate on feeling the movement of the correct diagonal. After a while, the posting diagonal will either feel right to you or it won't. Keep practicing until you're able to tell.

When you're confident of your ability to do the rising trot, and if your horse remains calm, try trotting for short stretches during your trail rides. You don't need to post on any particular diagonal; just make sure that you change every so often. Your horse will appreciate it.

12

The Sitting Trot

Most beginning riders react to being told they will learn the sitting trot by moaning, "I can't do that!" I promise that you'll not only learn to do it, you'll learn to like it. You must be able to sit to the trot before you can canter, and once you learn how, you'll find it easier to sit down through transitions. And if you get a chance to look over some dressage tests, you'll notice that at the higher levels the rising trot is no longer required. The rising trot was simply a means of helping the horse maintain his balance while you were finding yours.

You may find that sitting to the trot is easier than posting to it, because by now you're familiar with what it feels like. But until you can do the rising trot correctly, don't even attempt the sitting trot. Instead, go back and practice some more.

In the sitting trot you don't absorb the horse's movements through your seat. You don't just sit there and take it. Your seatbones stay firm and quiet in the saddle, without moving, and the jolts are taken up by your stomach and back. Your back is flexible, but it remains straight.

The best way to approach the sitting trot is through some simple exercises. The first one you know already, because you did it at the walk.

Tie a knot in the reins and ask your horse for a calm, easy, rhythmic trot. Then hold your dressage whip in front of you in both hands and raise your arms straight over your head, slightly behind the vertical, so that your upper body is leaning slightly backward. Sit down in the saddle. *Don't* roll forward into your thighs. Sit relaxed with your seatbones in the deepest part of the saddle, your shoulder blades closed and flush with your back, and concentrate on feeling the motion of the trot through your stomach and the small of your back. Try to absorb the motion in those two parts of your body. Your thighs, knees, and feet should be in the correct position, with your heels down. Since most beginning riders try to hunch forward at the sitting trot, this exercise will help you with your balance. Keep stretching *up*, so that you can feel the stretch in your hips, your stomach muscles, your rib cage, and your chest, but especially your stomach. Pretend you're a belly dancer and *move* with that motion. Don't try to clamp with your knees and absorb the jolts through your knees, or you'll start bouncing. And don't try to balance your weight on your stirrup irons. You'll find that this doesn't "balance" you at all, and in fact will push you right up out of the saddle.

It may help if you count "up-down, up-down," in the two-beat rhythm of the trot. On the "up," your stomach muscles push out, then stretch up and in. As they stretch in, you're coming "down," and you absorb the "down" motion with the small of your back.

Next, hold both reins in your inside hand. With your other hand, get a good grip on the pommel, straighten your arm, and push your shoulders away from your hand. You've done this exercise before too. You're stretching the front of your body upward and back as far as you can, and you'll realize that your seat remains very firm and still in the saddle. You'll clearly feel that the movements of the trot are being taken by your stomach and the small of your back. This exercise will help you maintain your seat at any gait, and will help you to move in harmony with the horse's rhythm. When you feel that you're balanced and moving with your horse, take up the reins again, holding your arms and wrists in the correct position, and sit through the trot once or twice around the ring. After you've practiced this a few times, do other exercises, or you might begin to rely on holding on to the saddle.

Here's the last and possibly the best exercise. Hold your reins in the normal position, cross your stirrups over the pommel of the saddle, and ask your horse to trot. Keep your back straight and your shoulder blades closed. Relax. Don't pinch your buttocks together, and don't clench your stomach muscles. Concentrate on absorbing the motion of the trot through your stomach and back.

I've introduced the sitting trot at this point mainly to prepare you for the canter, because you can't ask for the canter from a rising trot. Most horses need more help in striking off into the canter than you can give them by using your legs alone. You'll have to aid him with your back and seat, and you can't do that when you're posting because you don't have sufficient contact with the horse.

But at this point in your training, all your work at the trot should still be done at the rising trot. When you're not working on anything in particular, or if you sense your horse is getting bored and could do with a chance of pace, practice the sitting trot by going through the few exercises that I've just described.

Once you can sit to the trot easily and comfortably, you'll want to be able to influence and steady the horse's rhythm the way you did at the walk and the rising trot. Use both legs together, but rather than aid by footfall or stride, you'll have to do it by timing. Some horses, the lazy ones, will probably need the leg aid every stride. Others will need it only every other stride.

You will recall that in the beginning of this section I defined "forward" as meaning "with a longer, more rhythmical stride." It also means that the horse is moving willingly on from your leg with a rounded back and lively, energetic strides. But the horse won't do it by himself. You have to ask him to move forward by using your leg aids, and he will respond by stepping farther underneath himself with his hind legs and moving with increased impulsion.

Remember: forward does *not* mean faster.

Work your horse alternately at the walk and trot until he's relaxed and moving calmly but energetically forward into your hands. When this happens, he'll begin to reach for contact with the bit by stretching his neck forward and down. Let him. Don't try to pick his head up, and don't "give him his head" and ride with no contact at all. You *want* his head and neck long, and you want to be able to feel his mouth.

At this point the horse will probably begin moving the bit around in his mouth, chewing on it and perhaps foaming a little. That's a very good sign to watch for: the horse is showing you that he's not afraid of the bit or of your hands.

By now you should begin to feel that things are coming together—your own balance coupled with what your horse has learned on the lunge line. Like that old "head bone connected to the neck bone" song, you should begin to feel that every part of your body really is connected to every other part, and that all of you—through your balance, through your confidence in your horse—is connected to your horse as well.

13
The Canter

After all that you've learned so far, the canter—which once seemed so fast and difficult to control—will probably seem very anticlimactic. With most horses, the canter is a very easy gait to sit to. The only problem you'll have in the beginning is a tendency to bounce, and since you now have a good, balanced seat, all you have to keep in mind is to move your seat in a scooping motion as you follow the horse's movements. This "scooping motion" is very similar to the movement your hand makes as you dig out a ball of ice cream with an ice cream scoop—your seat moves down, forward, and up as you rotate your hips.

The real problem will be the one presented by your horse: how to get him from a sitting trot into a canter on the correct lead. If you allow your horse to canter on the wrong lead, he's going to be unbalanced. He'll rush off, you'll bounce, and neither of you will learn anything. You want him to do two things: strike off into a canter, and strike off with his outside hind leg, so that he's cantering with the inside foreleg leading.

First, make sure that you keep a light contact from your hands to the horse's mouth. Don't tighten the reins or try to shorten them. Keep the contact light, without slack, and keep an equal contact with both hands. Ask your horse for an easy, rhythmical trot, and sit to the trot once or twice around the ring. If his training on the lunge line has been sufficient, your horse may be able to move off into the canter directly from the walk. But what will probably happen is that he'll speed up into a rough, hurried trot and then canter. It's best to nip this habit in the bud and ask the horse for a canter from a calm, rythmical sitting trot from the very beginning. Use the full dimensions of the ring for your work on the canter; in other words, take your horse along the rail. And until you're sure that your horse is responding to your aids, ask him for the canter as you're approaching one of the short ends of the ring. You have two corners coming up. If he doesn't strike off at the first corner, you can try again at the second.

If you're trotting around the ring on your right rein, you want the horse to take his right lead. As you approach the corner, your horse's body will be slightly bent in the direction he's moving to—in other words, to the right. He must *remain* bent to the right as you ask for the strike-off into the canter. Never turn your horse's head to the outside. I don't care how many people have told you that this is the way to do it. This is not how you do it in dressage. Beginning riders are often taught to pull their horse's head to the outside because this throws the horse slightly off balance and forces him to take the lead with his inside foreleg. In dressage you don't "force" the horse to do anything; you let him use his own natural balance. It should be obvious to you that your horse cannot remain rounded to the right if you pull his head out. Your horse must strike off at the canter with his head, neck, and spine bending in the direction he's going to, and he's going to the right.

To ask for the canter on the inside lead, keep your inside leg at the girth, and move your outside leg back a few inches behind the girth. Your hands stay in a straight line to the horse's mouth and your elbows stay at your sides. Don't shorten your outside rein. With your inside rein, squeeze your fingers as if you were squeezing water out of a sponge. This squeeze-and-relax motion is a refinement of the same give-and-take motion that you've been using ever since you started work on the lunge line. It will help to keep the horse bent to the inside. At the same time that you squeeze your inside rein, aid with your inside leg at the girth by bringing your heel against his side. You might have to turn your toe out a little. Your inside leg is the most important one, since you ask for impulsion with it. Be sure to use it right at the girth. If you aid behind the girth, you'll push the horse's hindquarters out toward the rail. At the same time that you aid with your inside leg by using strong, short nudges, ask with your voice, using the same voice aid that you did on the lunge line. Either sit up straight in a normal, balanced position or lean back slightly from your hips. If you lean forward you'll displace the horse's weight into his forehand, and instead of cantering he'll probably rush off into a faster trot.

To ask for the canter on the inside lead, in other words, you will have to do four things more or less at the same time. It will help if you go over what these four things are and memorize them before you actually ask your horse for the canter. One: move your outside leg behind the girth and hold it there, with minimal "restraining" pressure. Two: nudge with your inside heel at the girth. Three: squeeze the inside rein with your fingers. Four: ask with your voice aid. If your horse was balanced and trotting rhythmically, he should strike off into the canter. If he doesn't, wait for the second corner and ask again.

It may take a day or two before your horse understands what you want him to do and actually canters. Don't lose your temper, and don't spend your whole training session asking him to canter. Do other things. Ask for transitions and halts and circles and the rising trot. Then do a sitting trot and ask for the canter again. Your horse is not refusing to canter in order to spite you. He's refusing to canter because he doesn't understand that that's what you want him to do. Continue to ask him on corners, because if he's going around a corner, he has to bend. Use your seat more firmly

A good canter on the left lead. The horse is balanced and moving forward. (*Photo by John Havey.*)

by leaning back in the saddle so that your seatbones will help push him forward, and use your legs a little more strongly. (And if you use your inside leg more strongly at the girth, you must exert an equal pressure with your outside leg.) Since you're also urging your horse forward with your voice, eventually he will have to canter. He won't know how else to respond to your aids *except* by cantering.

Your horse might find it especially hard to strike off into a canter on his stiff side, but through training on the lunge line he shouldn't have much trouble with his stiff side any- more—unless you were soft on him and let him canter in the direction he was happiest in. If your horse does prefer one side to the other it will be especially noticeable at the canter. Don't continue cantering him on the lead that feels the most comfortable to you, because it's the other lead your horse needs work on.

When he begins to canter, praise him. Praise him using your voice, and at the same time look at his inside shoulder to see if he's gotten the correct lead. You know from the lunge line that the shoulder that stretches up and forward more than the other—and consequently the foreleg that reaches farther forward than the other—is the leg he's leading with. Reward him first, even if it turns out that he's on the wrong lead. At least he's cantering, and that's half the battle.

If he's on the correct lead, let him take about 10 strides around the ring and praise him with your voice the whole time. If he's on the wrong lead, don't bring him down immediately. This would only scare him and make him think that he was wrong to respond to your aids by cantering—that you wanted something else. Even if he's disunited (and you'll know if he is because his backbone will feel as though it's separating), let him take two or three strides and then ask for the trot by using your voice aid, "trot" or "HO-ho," or whatever you've been doing, and at the same time moving your fingers in a very easy give-and-take on the reins, the squeezing-the-sponge movement. Let him trot, and sit to it, until he's moving evenly and calmly. When he gets to another short corner, ask him again.

If your horse tries to go faster at the trot before he goes into the canter, don't let him get away with it. Bring him back to a steady, even trot, and ask him again, leaning back slightly so that your seat is firmly in the saddle and helping him to go forward. If your horse still keeps trying to trot faster, shorten your reins slightly so that you have a little more contact with his mouth, and then put them into your inside hand. With your outside hand, grasp the pommel and push your upper body back away from your hand so that you're sitting deep in the saddle, the same way you did when you were learning to sit to the trot. Then ask for the canter with your voice and legs at the same time that you push forward with your seat. Move with the horse and drive him into the canter with your seat and back.

If your horse understands what you want and refuses to canter because he's lazy, aid your leg with the whip. (Remember that your whip is in your inside hand.) If he doesn't move off immediately when you ask for the canter, ask again, and at the same time that you ask with your legs, ask with the whip. Never use the whip to punish your horse because he's not cantering. If your horse is afraid of the whip, you haven't gained anything. In fact you've lost something—his confidence in you.

Eventually your horse will get it right. He may surprise you and get it right straight off. When he does strike off on the correct lead, make sure that you're going large and using the whole ring. Don't canter your horse in a circle, no matter how big you think it is, because he'll tire. And don't let him canter for more than a dozen strides before you bring him down to the trot. He's used to cantering from his work on the lunge line, but he's not used to cantering with you on his back. Only canter him two or three times during a training session. When he's sure of your aids, and sure of his own balance, you can work him at the canter on circles and for progressively longer periods of time, but don't rush it, because your seat probably won't be that good yet either.

When you want to change leads, bring the horse down to a trot. Change rein through the diagonal, and when you come to the first short corner of the opposite side, ask for the canter again.

As a rider, your concern is with your position in the saddle when you ask for the canter, while you're at the canter, and as you're asking for a transition back to the trot or (as you get better at it) the walk. You want to move in harmony with the horse; you want to be balanced. Although you must move your legs to ask for the strike-off, the rest of your position doesn't change. You don't grip with your knees; you don't do anything that you wouldn't do at the walk. Your back remains straight, your shoulders are flat, and there's a straight line running from your elbows through the reins to the horse's mouth.

During the canter, the only thing you're doing the least bit differently is moving your seat in the scooping motion I described earlier: push down with your spine and seatbones, then forward into the saddle toward your hands, then up—down, forward, and up as you follow the one-two-three, one-two-three rhythm of the canter. Once you've realized you don't have to work quite so hard to keep your seat, you can sit still in the saddle and begin using your back and stomach muscles more than your back and your seatbones. In the beginning, however, you should concentrate on pushing with your seat to drive the horse forward. By "scooping" in this way you're actually encouraging him to use his hindquarters with more energy and impulsion.

When you first ask for a downward transition from the canter you may find that your horse comes down into a strong, fast trot that's nearly impossible to sit to. I suggest to my students that while their horse is still cantering they put the reins in their inside hand and hold the pommel with their outside hand. Then I tell them that if they stretch their upper body away from their hand and push their seat deeper into the saddle, they won't bounce. (And curb any inclination to shove your feet forward and brace yourself with your stirrups, or to hang on with your knees. Your legs shouldn't move at all.) At the same time, use your voice to soothe your horse and slow him down.

When you ask for a downward transition, especially if you use "ho-ho" as your voice aid, don't let your horse come to an instant, utter stop. Use your legs to bring him down smoothly to the trot, and make sure that he keeps trotting.

This rider is doing the hands-over-head exercise, and her horse is leaning in on the circle. The rider has let her right hip collapse and as a result is forced to keep her balance by gripping with her legs. (*Photo by George Wrightson.*)

Don't let him die on you. Later, when you bring him down to the walk from the canter, always bring him down *through* the trot.

After your horse has picked up the correct canter lead a few times, concentrate on feeling it. The canter lead is easier to feel than the posting diagonal. Try to determine which shoulder is moving the most. The shoulder the horse is leading with will be the one that feels as though it's bouncing your leg off the saddle. It will be harder for you to keep your leg close to the horse on that side. Once you have checked and know your horse is on the correct lead, concentrate on what it feels like. The next time, try to feel whether it's right before you look down. Soon you'll be able to tell what lead your horse is on just from the way it feels to you.

Once your horse has settled down and is cantering confidently and quietly, you want him to go forward at the canter the same way he does at the walk and trot. Ask him for longer, more regular strides by aiding with both legs together, the way you did at the sitting trot. Don't try to concentrate on individual footfalls; they're coming too close together. Instead, concentrate on the timing—the rhythm and tempo that you want—and ask every third beat of the stride: one-two-three, leg; one-two-three, leg.

You'll often hear that "forward" and "straight" are the two most important words in dressage. They are—but don't ask your horse to move forward at the canter until he's relaxed and balanced at all three gaits. And make sure that you take your horse's mental and physical preparedness into consideration. Lazy horses will need stronger, more frequent aids than high-strung ones. But if you push a high-strung horse forward too hard or before he's ready, you'll totally confuse him. He'll quicken his pace and instead of taking longer, more rhythmical strides he'll begin taking short, irregular, mincing ones with his head up in the air and his back hollow. Such a horse needs to be worked quietly and calmly until he's re-established his balance and his confi-

The horse is on his forehand and his head and neck are bent to the side, thus unbalancing him entirely. (*Photo by John Havey.*)

dence. If you know that your horse isn't very strong physically, don't keep after him to make him go forward, because he won't be able to do it. Respect his limitations and take your time. He'll probably go just as far and do just as well as any other horse, but you'll have to be more patient with him.

Although I haven't dealt in this section with exercises designed to make your horse more supple, he should be in much better physical shape than he was when you started. You've also probably noticed a corresponding change in his attitude; he's more willing to do what you ask. He has confidence in you, and he's responsive to your aids—your voice, your hands, your body. If you don't feel that your horse has improved in all these respects—if he's not relaxed with you, if he's not moving freely forward and reaching for a contact with the bit at all three gaits, if he hasn't achieved much impulsion—go back over everything you've taught him. Go back to your work on the lunge line. It could be that the horse didn't fully understand something before you went on to the next step. You can solve a surprising number of problems by going back to the lunge. Try to isolate exactly what's wrong. You may find that it lies with you, that you aren't really using your aids correctly, for instance, and that it's not the horse that's stiff or uncooperative or "stupid."

Don't push your horse to do more than he's capable of doing because *you're* impatient. Above all, don't be tempted to advance to higher levels of training until your horse understands what you want and does it willingly and easily every time you ask, because you'll only get yourself in trouble.

Now that your seatbones have stopped hurting you can extend your training sessions to three-quarters of an hour, but no more than that—and probably no longer than half an hour. Weak horses still can't take more than 15 or 20 minutes. Above all, don't bore your horse to death. Vary your lessons.

Colonel Alois Podhajsky, the former director of the Spanish Riding School, was once told by an employee of Madison Square Garden in New York City that of all the horses he had ever seen perform, only Podhajsky's Lippizaners looked happy. Your horse should enjoy what he's doing. Always end your training sessions from the saddle the same way you did on the lunge line—on a pleasurable, positive note, so that your horse looks forward to them. Through training you've probably found one particular exercise that your horse does better than all the rest. Finish your lesson by doing that one exercise, so you can praise your horse lavishly. He'll return to the barn in a very happy frame of mind, and both you and he can justifiably feel proud of yourselves.

Part Four
TRAINING FROM THE SADDLE– ADVANCED AIDS

14

Turns and Corners

By now you've learned that your basic position in the saddle never changes, no matter what you're doing. At all three gaits your head and back remain straight, your thighs are long, and your lower legs gently embrace the horse's sides; there is a straight line from your elbows to the horse's mouth. Because you've learned how to move one part of your body without moving any of the other parts, you can make smooth transitions from one gait to another without depending on the reins or jarring your horse's back.

Now, through an increasingly subtle application of your natural aids, you're going to ask your horse to engage his hindquarters and lighten his forehand with you on his back the same way he did on the lunge line. You'll ask him to use himself with increased energy and collection as he refines his gaits and makes even smoother transitions. In addition, you'll begin gymnasticising your horse to strengthen him physically and make him even more responsive to your aids.

At this point I'm going to stop relying on the horse's gaits to teach you. What you have to understand now is that there are specific aids you use to ask for a specific response at *any* gait. You ask the horse to make a circle at the canter the same way you do at the trot, and you ask for a half-halt at the trot the same way you do at the walk. But I suggest that you practice first at the walk. The walk is slow and easy to sit to while you figure out which hand, leg, etc., goes where and how firmly you'll need to "ask" before the horse responds. Once you can use your aids at the walk automatically, without thinking about each step, practice at the faster gaits.

The first thing I want you to do is take off the side reins. You won't need them anymore.

Next, I'm going to ask you to take a good look at the way your horse is carrying his head. At this stage of training, his head and neck should look quite long to you. Ideally, he should be carrying his head on a slightly higher level than his body, and from your perspective, on his back, his poll should look a little bit higher than his withers. Notice that I said "ideally." If the horse looks and feels relaxed to you, then his head carriage is correct no matter where it is. Let him find his own position. What is most important is that he's going forward willingly with his back rounded and his gaits rhythmic and lively, and he knows better than you do how he can accomplish this. If you attempt to set the position of his head with your hands you still haven't understood the true meaning of the word "forward."

But if your horse is dropping his head down so low you're afraid he'll kick himself in the chin, he's either so bored he's ready to fall asleep or else he's lazy. Don't try to pull his head up by pulling on the reins. Change gaits, or change rein and go in the other direction, or increase the tempo of the gait and ask for a bit more liveliness. At the end of this chapter I've included a few exercises that will wake him up and make him think about what he's doing.

On the other hand, if your horse is raising his head (and thus hollowing his back), he's telling you that he's not relaxed. Make sure you're not the cause of his unhappiness. Check to see that you aren't snatching at his mouth or balancing yourself on the reins. You should feel only a light contact with the bit. Loosen your reins to get lighter contact, and calm your horse down by talking to him and stroking his neck, one hand at a time, the way you've been doing, until he relaxes and takes a quiet contact with the bit. When

The horse is going forward towards the rider's hands with a rounded back and a lowered head and neck. (*Photo by George Wrightson.*)

he's relaxed and feels confident that you're not going to jar his mouth, his head will come down.

What I've just said applies to trail rides too. Your horse should be going willingly forward in a calm, relaxed manner, with a rounded back and a long neck. He shouldn't be stargazing or yanking the reins out of your hands.

From your work on the lunge line you know that a lateral bend is when your horse bends, throughout his whole body, along the curve of a circle so that his hind feet follow the track of his front feet. He should bend exactly the same way with you on his back. The next time you ride through a corner of the ring, begin thinking about that corner as part of a circle, which it actually is. (I'll go into greater detail con-

The horse is correctly bending his entire body to the curve of the circle, although he's slightly overbent (his head is behind the vertical). (*Photo by George Wrightson.*)

cerning circles in Chapter 17, Gymnasticising Your Horse.) Your horse should not only be looking around the corner with his head and neck as he rides through it, he should be bending the entire length of his body around the arc of the turn.

There's a very practical reason for asking the horse to bend throughout his body when you're going through a corner. Suppose you're out riding in the country and you want to turn down a particular trail. If you ask your horse to turn by using only your inside rein, he's perfectly capable of bending his neck around until he's nibbling on the toe of your boot and sauntering right past the turn. It's called "rubbernecking."

You achieve a lateral bend by using your *outside* rein, your inside seatbone, and both your legs—in addition to your inside rein.

Let's take the aids one at a time.

Outside rein. Your outside rein keeps the horse from turning his head too far to the inside. Equally important, it also influences the horse's haunches by encouraging him to step farther underneath himself as he rounds the corner. You want a firm, steady contact with the outside rein at all times, so that the horse can feel it.

Inside rein. Your inside rein only influences the position of the horse's head and neck. But now, instead of simply opening your inside rein to ask for the turn, squeeze it. "Take" the rein with a short, elastic squeeze and then let go—"give"—by tightening and then relaxing the muscles of your wrist and hand. This movement is identical to the "squeezing-a-sponge" movement you used in lunging, where you flexed your hands downward from the wrist and simultaneously squeezed your fingers. The contact should be very light, much lighter than with your outside rein. When you "give," the contact will be almost slack. When you "take," you'll feel a slightly stronger contact. The position of your hands stays the same, however—thumbs uppermost with your wrists bent in the direction of the horse's opposite ear. Be especially careful not to turn your hand over as you give-and-take with the inside rein. Time the squeezes to the horse's strides. In general, as long as your horse continues to move forward in a relaxed and willing manner, give-and-take with every other stride at all three gaits.

Outside leg. Your outside leg rounds and steadies the horse's hindquarters and keeps him from swinging his haunches to the outside. Use your outside leg a few inches behind the girth. (The exact distance depends on the angle of the turn, and is something you'll be better able to judge with experience.) If you're at the walk, use your legs alternately, first the inside leg, then the outside. At the trot and canter use them both together.

Inside leg. Your inside leg asks for the bend the same way your hand would "ask" your own body to bend at the waist if you pushed there. It also asks for impulsion. At the walk, use your inside leg at the girth every time the *horse's* inside leg comes down to the ground. (And if you can't tell when the horse's inside hind leg comes down, shame on you. Go back to Basic Aids.) Nudge the horse's side by squeezing gently with your calf and ankle.

Inside seatbone. You use your inside seatbone to add more weight to the horse's inside hind leg, and you do it by sitting more deeply into the saddle with your inside seatbone. Don't cock your hip and rock to the inside. Your body should stay straight, although when you weight your inside seatbone your inside leg will sink down a little farther into the stirrup iron. In order to support this added weight, the horse must bring his inside leg farther under his body. This, in turn, will enable him to move forward with even greater impulsion.

Now let's put them all together. You're going along the rail at a walk and you're approaching a corner. As you reach it, squeeze gently with your inside rein and then let go to ask for the bend. With your outside rein, increase the contact by not allowing your arm to slip forward. "Hold" the rein with your hand and arm in the correct position and your fingers closed on the rein; don't let the horse pull your arm forward as he turns. Weight your inside seatbone and aid with your inside leg at the girth every time the horse sets his inside hind leg down to ask for impulsion. Keep the horse's hindquarters correctly rounding on the turn and following the track of his forehand by moving your outside leg behind the girth and squeezing alternately with your inside leg.

Be sure to exert the same amount of pressure with your legs that you do with your reins, and use both only as strongly as you need to. If you use too much rein and not enough leg, the horse will try to slow down. You *must* maintain the rhythm of the gait throughout the turn so the horse doesn't become unbalanced. If you use too much leg, the horse may mistake what you want and break into a canter. The aids are very similar, but you should be using your inside leg quite a bit more energetically to ask for the canter than you do to ask for a lateral bend.

If your horse does canter, use your voice aid and quiet pats on the neck to bring him back to the trot. (And from now on I want you to use only your *inside* hand to stroke his neck. Keep a firm, steady contact with your outside rein; don't let it go slack.) The next time you ask for a bend don't use your legs quite so vigorously. "Hold" your legs passively, with just enough pressure so the horse can feel the shape of the bend and know that you want him to keep going forward.

Practice riding your circles using the same aids: both reins, both legs, and your inside seatbone. But don't try circles any smaller than 40 feet in diameter yet. Your horse still isn't supple enough to handle them comfortably.

Now you've begun asking for two quite different responses from the horse with your two reins, and it's the action of the outside rein through the horse's body that connects all the other aids. Through the influence of your inside leg, the horse will begin working into that steady outside rein contact and engaging his hindquarters more actively. The squeezing-the-sponge movement of your inside rein will help to relax him. As the bit moves softly in his mouth, without bumping him or hurting him, he'll begin to open and close his mouth as he starts chewing on the bit. Some horses will begin to foam a little, or salivate. These are all good signs to watch for, because they indicate the horse isn't afraid of the bit or of your hands. You should gradually begin to feel as though your horse's back is rounding underneath you, particularly on corners, from the influence of your outside rein and inside leg. You might also feel a little more flexion in the horse's poll.

If you're using a dropped noseband, loosen it a hole or two to encourage the horse to move the bit around in his mouth.

Whatever else you do, keep the horse moving forward. Without that you don't have anything. Make sure that the rhythm of the walk doesn't change and that you continue to move your back and seat very slightly backward and forward as you follow the horse's movements. When you progress to the trot and canter, be sure to maintain the rhythm of the gait with your body so that the horse can feel it.

At this point I want to introduce a few more exercises, but these are for your horse, not for you. They'll encourage him to be more attentive to the bend you're asking him for, and they'll also encourage him to use his hind legs more actively under his body.

First, lay some boards at right angles in the short ends of the ring to make yourself some genuine square corners. If you already have a rectangular ring you're one step ahead of the game.

Next, using the full dimensions of the ring, mentally draw a big X through it. The center of the X will be the center of the ring. Ride your horse at a walk down one of the long sides of the ring, straight along the rail, for a few strides. Then gradually work your horse in toward the center of the ring, keeping him *straight*. Don't ask him to bend, and don't turn him on a diagonal facing the opposite corner. Continue to move him toward the center of the ring, keeping his backbone parallel to the long side of the rail the whole time. You want to end up in the middle of that imaginary X.

I'm deliberately not telling you how to do this exercise. You should be able to figure it out for yourself if you think about the effect of your outside rein and how your legs influence the horse's hindquarters.

But if you're really having trouble, take a quick look at Chapter 17 and the discussion of leg-yields. But I don't want you to do a full-fledged leg-yield yet. What I want you to do is concentrate on using your leg aids to move the horse sideways instead of forward while your contact with both reins remains steady and even. Don't influence with your reins any more than that.

When the horse reaches the cross in the X, move him back to the same side of the ring that he left from, again keeping his back parallel to the rail. Get him back to the rail in time for the next corner, so the horse can take two or three strides along the rail before you ask him to bend around the corner. When your horse is relaxed and able to do this exercise correctly and without resistance, try it at the trot. Do *not* try it at the canter.

For the next exercise, draw an imaginary line down the center of the ring and parallel to the two long sides. What you want to do is make a series of S-curves, or loops, down the ring. Picture a dollar sign. The slash is your imaginary line. You ride back and forth across it so that the first loop is on one side of it, the second loop is on the opposite side, and the third loop is on the same side as the first.

Start on your imaginary line on the short side of the ring and mentally divide the ring into thirds. Leave the rail at the walk and make your first loop. When you reach the center line you should be a third of the way down the ring. Cross the center line and finish the S by going toward the opposite rail, then loop back to the center line again. When you reach the center line you should be two-thirds of the way down the ring. Make your third loop toward the opposite end of the imaginary line. When you reach it, halt.

You have just done a serpentine in three loops.

You ask the horse for the bend by using both reins, both legs, and your inside seatbone. When your horse understands what you want of him and goes willingly forward, ask for the serpentine at the trot. Remember to change posting diagonals every time you cross the center line, because your outside diagonal will change every time you change direction.

When you're sure your horse is ready, ask for this exercise at the canter. Be sure to come down to the trot as you cross the center line in order to change leads.

The figure-8 is another very good suppling exercise. Ride your figure-8's so that each one is as long and as wide as the ring. Again, start from the center line on the short side and make a big half-circle, so that you return to the center line halfway down the ring. In dressage, a figure-8 has a straight line in the middle of it. When you reach the center line, straighten your horse for a few strides. Then change direction by changing the bend and make a complete circle using the whole second half of the ring. As you approach the center line again, straighten your horse, cross over the center line, and make a half-circle to finish the figure-8 where you began it, on the center line of the short side.

Since the figure-8 is such a useful exercise, I'll explain it in detail at this point so you'll know exactly what you should be doing.

Let's say you've been going along the rail to the right. As you ride through the first corner of the short side, the horse will be looking and bending to the right. When you've come two or three horse's lengths past the corner, begin your figure-8. Ride through the second corner as though it were the beginning of a circle; that's the degree of bend you ask for with your inside rein and outside leg. Use a very light give-and-take with your inside rein. Maintain a firm, even contact with your outside rein to encourage the horse to engage his hindquarters. Weight your inside seatbone. Reinforce the rhythm and tempo of the gait by aiding with your legs, your inside leg at the girth to influence the bend and ask for impulsion, and your outside leg behind the girth to steady the horse's haunches.

As you approach the center line, straighten your horse.

First, move your right leg slightly behind the girth. You want both legs behind the girth so you can control the horse's hindquarters and make sure they're directly behind his shoulders. Next, ask your horse to go from a left outside rein contact to a right outside rein contact. You do this by transferring him directly from one rein to the other without any break. Don't drop the contact with the left outside rein and then pick it up with the right one. Do it smoothly, without jerking the horse's mouth.

As you cross the center line, keep the horse straight for a couple of strides, so you can feel equal contact with both reins, and feel that the horse's hindquarters are in line with his forehand. Begin the second half of your figure-8 by completing the transfer of the horse to the right outside rein and by moving your left leg up to the girth. Now ride another half-circle.

If you've judged the dimensions of your circle accurately, you'll be able to cross the center line at the far end of the ring and complete your circle. If you didn't judge it accurately, you'll either find yourself short of the rail (which means your half-circle was too small) or cutting in sharply to avoid running into the rail (which means your half-circle was too big).

As you approach the center line again, straighten your horse for a few strides and transfer him smoothly from a right outside rein contact to a left one as you move your right leg up to the girth (your left leg will be behind the girth). Complete your half-circle, and the second circle of your figure-8, where you began it.

Practice figure-8's first at the walk, then at the sitting and rising trot, then at the canter. Be sure to come down to a walk or trot every time you change direction. Make sure you're giving the horse the correct aids, not too forcefully and at the right time, and are asking for just the right degree of bend to produce nice, fat, *round* figure-8's.

15
Increasing the Impulsion

If you look at your horse head on, you'll notice that his shoulders are much narrower than his hips. When he's going along the long side of the rail, his shoulders should be farther away from the rail than his hips are. If they are, he's straight—his spine is parallel to the rail and his hind feet are tracking into the steps of his forehand.

If the horse's inside shoulder and inside haunch are the same distance from the rail, he's crooked. Simply because of the way they're built, most horses would rather go along the rail with their hindquarters slightly to the inside, so that they're leaning in on the rail. The forehand is on one track and the hindquarters are deviating to the inside on a completely different track.

Let's say you're on the rail going to the right, as in the photograph. The horse is crooked; he's leaning in on the rail. To straighten him, you have to bring his forehand in slightly from the rail. Here is how you do this. First, use your left leg firmly at the girth to ask for more impulsion. Second, move your right leg slightly behind the girth to move the horse's hindquarters back toward the rail. Since the horse is bending his haunches to the inside—and he shouldn't be—you need to use your inside leg to straighten him. With your right, or inside, rein keep a light, steady contact. With your left rein use an elastic give-and-take. If you exert a steady pull, the horse will resist by pulling back. You want him to yield on that side so that he relaxes and offers you a softer contact. Once that happens, the horse's head and neck will come "in" to your inside rein, he will be stepping into (or overstepping) the track of his front legs with his hind legs, and his entire spine will be parallel to the rail from nose to tail.

The exercises I described in the preceding chapter will all help a crooked horse. Here's another one, which is a general all-round suppling exercise.

As you're going down the long side of the rail to the right, ask the horse to bend his whole body, from haunches to nose, very slightly around your inside leg. The aids you use to ask for the bend are the same ones you use to ask for a corner, although you don't apply them as strenuously. In other words, you want the left (outside) side of the horse's body to be slightly longer than the right side of his body. You have the correct amount of bend when the horse is looking very slightly to the right, just enough so that you can see his inside eyelashes. The horse should still be going forward equally into both reins and not drifting in toward the center of the ring.

Then do the same exercise going down the rail to the left, so the horse is bent around your inside leg, looking to the left and moving his haunches to the left.

You'll probably find that the horse resists bending (especially bending his neck) in one direction, but, going the other direction, he bends quite readily. As you may remember, he did almost the same thing on the lunge line—he has a favorite direction. For simplicity's sake, let's say he prefers going to the right and resists going to the left, because this is usually the way it works. You should practice bending him around your leg going to the left *because* he resists on that side; he needs to use himself more, to stretch on that side. Be sure that you continue to give-and-take with your inside rein. If you simply pull back on the rein because the horse is resisting you, he'll resist even harder, and he's stronger than you are. You want him to loosen up and yield to you on that

Hilda Gurney on Ahoy going straight at the canter.

Ahoy leaning his shoulder in on the rail and going crooked. His left fore is on one track, his right fore and left hind are on a second track, and his right hind is on a third track. (*Photos by Hillair Evans-Bell.*)

side, and if you continue to use an elastic give-and-take on the rein, his jaw will gradually relax and he'll offer you a softer contact.

At this point I can hear some of you grumbling, "So the horse leans in on the rail—big deal." It *is* a big deal. Most horses go crooked, and most riders let them. At this point in your horse's training he must be absolutely straight, because if he's not, this is as far as you're going to get in dressage. Your horse has to move straight forward at all three gaits, with his hindquarters directly in line with his forehand so that he can engage his hindquarters more actively and begin using himself with more impulsion. Advanced work is simply not possible unless your horse is straight.

In the preceding chapter I asked you to start thinking of a corner as part of a circle. Now I want you to begin riding each corner as though it was one quarter of a circle with a diameter of 40 feet—not through any particular love of symmetry but because it's good practice. It's very, very difficult to ride a corner keeping your horse bent exactly to the circumference of a 40-foot circle. It's also an excellent test of whether you're using your aids correctly and how responsive your horse is to them, which is why it's required in dressage competition.

First, locate your circle. Starting from the corner point, measure 21 feet down the long side. Then measure 21 feet down the short side. (You'll be riding approximately one foot off the rail.) Then draw a line into the ring from both points until the lines intersect. That point is the center of your imaginary circle. Mark it with a rock or something you can see easily and stay 20 feet away from that point *at all times*. Then mark a 20-foot line from that center point back into the corner. Where the line stops is the point you'll actually be riding over as you go through the corner. Mark all four corners of the ring the same way.

Prepare your horse for the corner before you actually begin riding through it. Let's say you're going along the rail

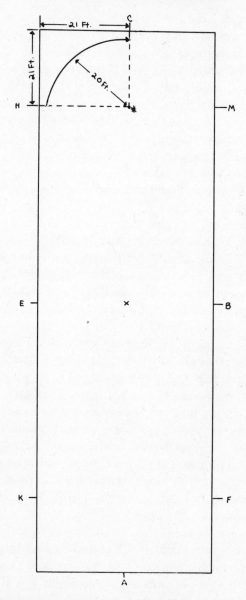

How to measure a corner. The asterisk marks the point of intersection that the rider keeps his eye on.

to your right. About two horse's lengths away from the first corner of the short side, prepare the horse for the turn: settle your inside seatbone into the saddle a little more firmly and move your outside leg slightly behind the girth; use your inside leg and inside rein to ask for the bend; hold with your outside rein.

Now work on refining your aids. As long as your horse is tracking straight and is willing to bend his body to the circumference of the corner without resisting, there's no need for you to give-and-take with your inside rein anymore. From now on you should maintain a light, even contact with both reins.

When the horse begins to turn, you'll notice that his outside, or left, shoulder is slightly in advance of his inside shoulder. Yours should be too, or you'll unbalance the horse. Turn from your hips so that you're looking into the center of your imaginary circle. Keep your back straight and your shoulders flush with your back. Don't simply twist your upper body around.

Be sure not to drop your right shoulder, or try to turn by shifting your weight to your outside stirrup (known as "collapsing your hip"). If you lean in and drop your shoulder, you're going to make the horse lean over and drop *his* shoulder. Remember that you should always be looking straight ahead between your horse's ears. When your horse is going to the right, he'll be looking to the right. If you concentrate on keeping your weight on your inside seatbone and turning from your hips, you won't exactly be looking between his ears anymore, but you and he will both be looking in the same direction—to the right.

As you ask for the bend around the corner, make sure that your outside rein maintains the same even contact, and that your arm doesn't slip forward. Your elbow stays at your side. Only your forearm should move as you direct your hand and wrist toward your inside (i.e., your opposite) hipbone. Keep your thumb uppermost and your wrist straight;

don't turn your hand over so that your knuckles are showing. And never cross your hand over the center line of the
mane. This movement will pinch the horse's tongue, since
the snaffle is jointed in the middle, and the horse will try to
evade your hand. The action of the outside rein comes from
your elbow, not your wrist or shoulder, but the elbow itself
doesn't move. Keep the contact with your inside rein steady
and light throughout the turn.

As your horse bends around the corner, what will probably happen is that his hindquarters will fall out—swing out
toward the rail—or that his inside shoulder will fall in.
Usually they happen together, and usually it's your fault.
You asked the horse to turn without preparing him. Let him
know what you're going to do by preparing your aids *before*
you ask for the turn. Also make sure that you're not giving
with the outside rein. The horse must be able to work into
that contact or he won't bend correctly.

After you've completed each exercise give your horse a
couple of good strong pats on the neck and let him go on a
loose rein for a few minutes. Allow the reins to slip through
your fingers all the way down to the buckle if you wish, but
don't let the horse pull the reins out of your hands.

After you've ridden through a few corners correctly,
change direction so you're tracking to the left. Although I've
dealt with the change of rein before, let me go over it in
more detail now.*

You're on the right rein, riding up the long side, and your
horse is straight. One or two horse's lengths before the first
short corner, prepare your horse for the turn. Ride through
the first corner, then ride through the second corner.
Straighten your horse and start down the long side. About
three yards past the second short corner ask your horse to
turn down the diagonal. Ride toward that same three-yards-

* If you ever ride a dressage test, what I'm giving you is the
correct way to change rein through the diagonal.

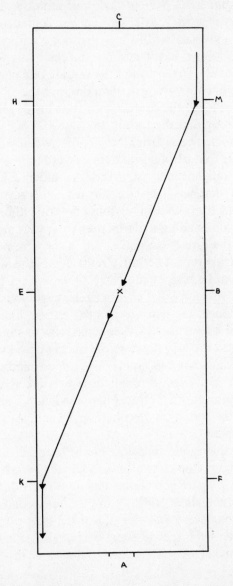

Change of rein across the diagonal, in an ordinary arena or a dressage
arena.

past-the-corner point on the opposite long side. The horse should be tracking straight, but he should be bent very slightly around your right leg and looking very slightly to the right because that's the way he came off the rail.

As you approach the center of the ring, straighten your horse for one horse's length. Then transfer him smoothly from a left outside rein contact to a right outside rein contact the way I told you when I explained the figure-8.

As you cross the center line the horse will be straight. Then ask him to bend very slightly around your left leg and look slightly to the left. By the time he reaches the rail he's prepared for the upcoming corner.

If you prefer, you can change rein through the circle. Although you'll never be asked to do it on a dressage test, it's good practice for your horse.

Say you're riding on a circle to your right. Begin a smaller circle within it and then describe an S that's exactly as big as the circle is. By the time you reach the perimeter of the circle again, you're tracking left.

You have sort of sneaked up on impulsion in these last two chapters by asking for it with your outside rein and inside leg through corners and the various movements I've asked you to do, and especially by your insistence that the horse track straight. Once you begin asking the horse to go absolutely straight down the long side of the rail and to bend according to the circumference of the circle when he's going through a turn, he *has* to begin using himself with impulsion, because you're not letting him be lazy and drift off on another track with his haunches anymore. He has to exert the joints and muscles of his hind legs to step directly underneath his body.

As you begin working at the trot and canter, make sure that the horse continues to move straight forward in the same even, steady rhythm. At the same time that you're thinking about seatbones and leg position and rein contact, make sure that the rhythm doesn't change. Your back and

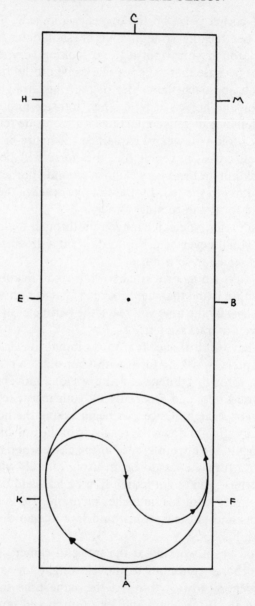

Change of rein through the circle.

seat should be moving with the horse in a very slight back-and-forth motion while your leg muscles squeeze and contract, squeeze and contract. Count out loud to maintain the rhythm, if you have to, or put a radio on the railing and play music to your horse. A metronome is another excellent aid, although a slightly monotonous one. No matter what you're doing, you should always have the feeling that the horse is moving forward from your legs into your hands and reaching for a contact with the bit—that he *wants* to go forward.

If you feel your horse losing impulsion and you apply your legs more strongly, the horse might misinterpret what you want and speed up. This is one mistake that isn't your fault. You have to use your legs for more impulsion, but if the horse thinks you want him to go faster, "hold" with both reins a little more strongly until the horse slows down and re-establishes his rhythm.

Now ask the horse to lengthen his stride a little more. When a horse lengthens his stride, he lengthens his entire frame. He doesn't go faster, he just takes longer steps. To do this, he has to move his hindquarters farther underneath himself and move with greater impulsion.

Ask for a lengthening of stride in a very quiet, relaxed manner. At the walk, gradually increase the pressure of your leg aids. When you aid with your left leg, keep it at the girth for half a second or so longer than you normally would before aiding with the right leg, and put a little more oomph into it. Don't kick. Begin to emphasize the movements of your back and seat a little as they follow the horse's movements. Exaggerate the back-and-forth movement of the walk by pushing the horse forward into your hands with the movements of your back and seat. At the same time, lower your hands so that the tops of your thumbs are level with the top of the horse's withers. When you begin to feel that the horse's back is rounding underneath you, almost growing, slowly let out the energy that you've created by relaxing your arms so that the horse can stretch his neck and back.

Don't let your arms stretch so far forward that they're straight out in front of you and your hands have lost contact with the horse's mouth. Your arms and hands slowly allow the horse to lengthen; you reach forward only slightly. You should still have a bend in your elbows and your elbows should still be at your sides, although they'll be slightly in front of your normal balanced seat position. Your arms provide the elasticity, the "give," that allows the horse to stretch and lengthen his entire frame.

Don't ask for a lengthening of stride for more than the length of the ring, and come back to a shorter stride any time you go through a corner.

To ask for a lengthening of stride at the trot, either a sitting or a rising trot, simply exaggerate the "up" movement of the trot and aid a little with your legs. If you're sitting, let yourself come up out of the saddle a little more; if you're rising, post a little higher. As you come up, lean back slightly, so that when you come back down you'll push the horse forward into your lowered hands. At the same time, your hands allow the horse to stretch forward, to lengthen his frame a little, and go on a slightly longer rein.

You ask for a lengthening of stride at the canter very nearly the same way you do at the trot. Increase the intensity of the "scooping" motion of your back and stomach muscles, and use your leg aids more strongly. Once you feel the horse's back rounding under you, let him slowly stretch forward into your lowered hands.

If you're still having trouble with your horse coming down from a canter into a rough, fast trot, it's because he's on his forehand. Ask for impulsion at the canter with your legs, and as you ask for the transition to the trot, post (without worrying about your diagonal) and continue aiding with your legs until the horse comes back to you. You're probably not preparing your horse adequately for the transition to the trot, and it's taken him by surprise. In the next chapter I'll tell you how to prepare your horse for transitions by

A very nice working trot with increased engagement and impulsion. (*Photo by John Havey.*)

A lengthening of stride at the trot. (*Photo by John Havey.*)

using the half-halt. A half-halt is a signal to your horse that you're going to do something different, and he'll prepare himself for whatever is coming up next by moving his hocks farther underneath his body in anticipation.

At the opposite end of the scale from lengthening of stride is collection. True collection isn't possible for a beginning horse any more than true extensions are, but both will result from the foundations you've already laid down. Collection requires a tremendous amount of impulsion, and the horse has to develop his muscles over a long period of time in order to move forward with lowered hindquarters, a raised and lightened forehand, and airy, animated steps.

Remember this: as you do all these movements, even the most willing horse will turn sour and uncooperative if you drill him over and over on the same routines day after day. If you sense he's getting unhappy, take him on a long, leisurely trail ride. Give him a few days off. And don't forget to ask yourself: whose fault is it *really* that he's getting so bored?

16
Getting the Horse on the Bit

A horse that's on the bit is moving forward in response to the rider's aids, or is "going to the aids." To an observer, such a horse appears to be moving energetically forward with lively, cadenced steps. His back is relaxed and rounded, he's carrying most of his weight on his hindquarters, and his forehand is slightly elevated. He no longer carries his neck long, but raised and flexed at the poll so that his face is slightly in front of a line perpendicular to the ground.

To the rider, who is more interested in the "feel" than in appearances, the horse will feel as though he's carrying himself without any support from the rider's hands. The contact is light and yielding; the rider feels as though his hands are joined to the horse's mouth by rubber bands. The horse responds to his lightest aid without stiffening or resisting in any way.

You ask your horse to go to the aids by asking him for a half-halt. I introduced the half-halt in Part Two, Training from the Ground, where I defined it as a barely visible pause in the gait that encourages the horse to engage his hindquarters. Half-halts help the horse to use his hind legs more energetically; in other words, you ask for a half-halt when you want more impulsion.

Although you should never ask for the half-halt while the horse is standing still, here's a little exercise which might give your horse some idea of what you'll be asking for. While he's at the halt, shorten up on your reins until you can

171

feel an even contact with his mouth. Then use your legs to ask him to walk forward. But don't let him actually start to move. "Hold" him with your arms and wrists.

Then try the half-halt at the walk. You're going along the rail, pushing the horse forward by squeezing alternately with your legs and letting your back and stomach follow the movements of his back so that he's constantly reaching for a contact with the bit. Remember the "frame" concept from lunging? On the lunge, your horse was framed between the whip and the lunge line. Now he's framed between your legs and your hands. As you ask for the half-halt, think about walking the horse into the front of that frame—your hands. The horse should *always* move forward from your legs toward your hands. You're not going to work backward by asking for the halt from your hands; you're not going to pull back on the reins. Picture the horse walking *forward* into a halt or half-halt, not down to a halt. (I'll discuss the full halt in detail in the following chapter.)

How you do it: as your legs urge the horse forward, pull your shoulder blades back, push your chest out, and sit down on your seatbones. Brace your back muscles; don't let yourself move back and forth with the horse anymore. (But don't stiffen to the point of rigidity.) Close your seatbones on the horse and "hold" your legs closed firmly around his sides. Stop moving with him. Then close your hands on the reins using short, firm, repeated movements. I hesitate to use the word "squeeze" here because the movement is more forceful and not as elastic as the give-and-take "squeezing-a-sponge" movement you've been using, and is much closer to the way you would clench your hand to make a fist. But you still use the same muscles in your wrists and hands and your hands still break from the wrist without turning over.

As you make yourself heavy and unresponsive to the horse's movements (the weight in your seatbones comes from your shoulders and uplifted chest), he'll start realizing that the weight on his back—you—isn't moving with him anymore. And he'll start to come to a halt.

But since you want a half-halt, as soon as the horse pauses—just before he comes down to a complete stop—ask him to walk on by relaxing your hands and wrists. Don't let your arms slip forward, and don't drop the reins. Ease up on the contact with his mouth by unclenching your hands. At the same time, resume the alternate squeezing with your legs and start moving with the horse again.

That's how it works in theory. In practice, you probably won't be able to ask your horse for a half-halt this way, because your horse probably still isn't taking an equal contact with both reins; most horses don't. Your horse probably has a favorite side, and as a result he responds differently to one rein than he does to the other—as you noticed when you were working to straighten him by bending him around your inside leg. On his stiff side you'll feel a firm contact with the rein, while your contact with the other rein feels soft or nonexistent. The horse's stiff side corresponds to his least favorite direction. He's reluctant to engage his hind leg on that side and use it underneath himself. The side with the soft contact is the horse's hollow side. It's called that because the horse will shift his hindquarters to that side (and thus hollow his body) in order to evade contact with the bit.

In other words, the horse is still reluctant to go straight. He *has* to take an equal contact with the bit: to soften and yield on his stiff side, and to accept the rein contact on his hollow side. Don't make the mistake of thinking that just because the horse is soft on one side that's what you want—it's not what you want. The contact is soft because the horse is evading your hand by falling behind the bit so that his hindquarters drift in and he's no longer tracking straight.

What you do in order to ask him to take an equal contact with the bit is use your rein in a forceful half-halt on his stiff side (and again I'm going to assume that his stiff side is his left side) and a softer half-halt on his hollow side. A forceful half-halt—the short, clenching-your-fist movement that I just described—will encourage the horse to yield to you, to relax, on his stiff side. A soft half-halt will encourage the horse to *accept* a contact.

You'll ask for more impulsion by aiding with your left leg at the girth. With your right leg you'll aid behind the girth to push the horse's hindquarters over so that he's stretching his body forward into that "hollow" right rein. Influence with your legs stride for stride with the horse's movements until you actually close your legs on him to ask for the half-halt.

Keep in mind that the half-halt is a pause in a single stride. There is one split second when the frame closes: your shoulders, your wrists, your seatbones, your legs are all closed. The next second you "give" again, and the horse completes his stride. The half-halt must never interrupt the horse's regular forward movement.

Now let's put everything together. As you're walking along the rail, take up your reins until you feel a light contact with the horse's mouth. You'll feel the horse begin to stiffen and resist on his left side and evade on his right.

Close your shoulder blades, lift your chest, and brace your back by sitting down on your seatbones. Stop aiding with your legs in the rhythm of the gait: move your right leg behind the girth, close your legs around the horse's sides, and leave them closed. Make a fist with your left hand by clenching your fingers (tighten your little finger first), flexing your wrist downward, and closing the muscles of your hand and arm. At the same time, give-and-take with your right hand using a softer action.

The horse will pause.

The instant he does, ease up on the rein contact by releasing first your little fingers, then your hands and wrists. Move your right leg up to the girth again and resume aiding with your legs in the rhythm of the gait. Begin moving with the horse again.

The horse is balanced and on the bit, going straight forward with a rounded back. (*Photo by John Havey.*)

Repeat the half-halts until the horse yields and goes forward with an even contact in both reins. You'll be able to feel it instantly because you'll feel his back and jaw muscles relax and see him begin to nod his head and neck slightly up and down. This nodding tells you he's taken an equal contact with the bit. The instant you feel that even, elastic contact in the reins, hold your hands quiet, so that the contact (especially the contact with the right, "hollow" side) remains fairly firm. Don't follow the nodding motion of his head with your hands and arms.

In the beginning your horse will probably go forward on the bit for only a half dozen steps or so, because he's not yet sure whether that's what you want. Then he'll stiffen again. Don't just hang onto that left rein and pull, because it won't

The horse is evading by nosediving his head into the ground. (*Photo by George Wrightson.*)

do you any good. Half-halt him more strongly on his stiff side and more softly on his hollow side until he accepts an equal contact with both reins and goes forward on the bit again for a few more strides. He'll probably continue trying to resist or evade your hands one way or another until he figures out that when he resists, you resist; but when he relaxes his jaw and poll and goes freely forward you relax too, and everything is very pleasant. Too many beginning riders make the mistake of thinking, "Oh-oh, my horse is fighting this, it must be wrong." Of course your horse will fight and stiffen up—he's never been asked to do this before. You have to be patient and work with him until he's certain of what you want.

Horses resist being asked to go to the aids in fairly pre-

The horse is evading the bit by raising his head and neck and hollowing his back. He's *above the bit. (Photo by John Havey.)*

dictable ways. I'm going to deal with the most common of these evasions now, and I want to stress that no matter what you do in the future—whether it's a leg-yield or a circle or you're just fooling around out on the trail—you deal with them in the same way.

If your horse is carrying his head too low. You'll feel that he's ready to nose-dive into the ground. You need to ask for more impulsion, and you do this by bracing your back muscles and bearing down with your seatbones. At the same time, use your legs strongly in the rhythm of the gait. Don't let them lie passively on the horse's side.

If you're trying to get your horse to take an equal contact in both reins by strong half-halts on the stiff side and your horse is also carrying his head too low, direct the action of the stiff-sided rein toward your *opposite* hip. And make sure your hand doesn't cross over the horse's mane.

If your horse is carrying his head too high. Your horse is **above the bit;** you'll see him poking his nose in the air and feel his back hollowing. To ask him to lower his head, direct the actions of the stiff-sided rein higher, toward your chest, on your right (or opposite) side. Once again, repeat the half-halts on both reins until the horse's back and jaws have relaxed and he's going forward with an even contact.

If your horse takes too strong a contact with both reins. You'll feel him trying to yank you out of the saddle. The problem is two-fold: his head is too low and he's leaning on the bit. Correct him with strong half-halts, using both reins, and by forcefully bracing the muscles of your back. Use your legs very lightly, however; just enough to keep in contact with his sides. What's probably happened is that you've created so much energy with your legs that you can't contain it in your hands—the frame idea again. Slowing the tempo will also help; so will a transition to another gait.

If your horse is overbent. This evasion is especially tricky because it's more difficult to detect than the others. When your horse is on the bit you should be able to see the crown of his head—the highest part of his forelock that falls forward between his ears. If you can only see his ears, and not the top of the forelock as it breaks over, your horse is probably overbent, or **behind the bit:** instead of carrying his head slightly in front of the perpendicular, his nose is tucked into his chest so that his face is behind the perpendicular. Use soft half-halts to encourage him to accept the bit, repeatedly offering a softer contact after each "hold" while using both legs to ask for more impulsion from the hindquarters.

By now you've probably figured out that the little straightening exercise I had you do to correct a horse that leaned in on the rail was essentially a half-halt on one rein,

The horse is *behind the bit*. (*Photo by John Havey.*)

although I didn't call it that. The problem at that point wasn't so much that the horse was stiff (although by leaning in on his shoulder he stiffened that side of his body), but that he was crooked.

From now on I'd like you to use half-halts to prepare your horse for transitions. Be especially careful, when you ask for a half-halt for a downward transition, that you ask with your hands very quietly, without pulling or jerking. Transitions are very difficult to do correctly. Very often you'll see the horse fling his head up, which means the rider asked with his hands too quickly or too hard, and wasn't pushing the horse forward into his hands.

Sometimes I even use half-halts to prepare my horse for a corner. Be sure to ask for a half-halt a horse's length before you start the bend.

You might find that one half-halt to prepare the horse isn't enough. How many times you ask for a half-halt depends on the gait and how much time you have. At a walk, you can ask on every stride until the horse responds to you. At a trot or canter you won't have time to ask more often than every other stride. You may find yourself asking for half-halts all the way through what you were trying to prepare the horse for. In general, half-halt the horse until you get what you want—which is balance and more impulsion.

Some of my beginning students always want to know how many inches or hand-spans to take up the reins so their horse is on the bit. Obviously I can't tell them. There are no ready-made formulas to measure the rein contact for "on the bit." What you want to feel is an elastic "connectedness" from your hands to the horse's mouth that is a result of the horse springing forward from your legs and yielding to your hands from his jaw and poll. The contact will vary from horse to horse, depending on his temperament, prior training, and a number of other factors. The only formula I can offer you is that as you ask for more impulsion, take up the reins until you feel a firm but yielding contact with the horse's mouth. (And once again I want to stress that your arms don't move back and forth as the horse nods his head. Your arms should be at your sides, not stiff, but not moving. Check the rest of your position from time to time too; don't let your seat fall all to pieces because you're concentrating on your horse.) This "connected" feeling is what you want to maintain for the rest of your work in dressage.

This is also the time my students will invariably ask me whether their horse should be on the bit even when they're out on the trail. I tell them that once their horse has learned to go on the bit he should be on the bit from the time they get into the saddle until the time they dismount. On the trail they don't need to ask for quite as much impulsion, but the horse should always be going forward to the bit with lively, energetic steps and a relaxed attitude.

17
Gymnasticising Your Horse

Now you're ready to begin gymnasticising your horse. Of course everything you've done so far has helped in loosening him up and developing his musculature. But these exercises, in particular, will build on your previous work by asking the horse for additional impulsion, and are particularly good for strengthening his hind legs, his shoulders, and his hips. A horse that's supple and in top physical form will find it very easy to respond to your lightest aid smoothly and brilliantly.

First of all, start riding in smaller circles—specifically, circles with a diameter of 33 feet. You're undoubtedly wondering how going around in circles will gymnasticise your horse. In the first place, it's far more difficult than it looks to execute a perfectly round circle—and circles *are* round. They aren't egg-shaped, and they don't have square corners or flat sides. A surprising number of people compete in upper-level dressage tests who can't ride a round circle. In the second place, asking a horse to bend his entire body to the circumference of a 33-foot circle is asking quite a lot of him physically, and he won't be able to do it unless he's relaxed and supple in every joint of his body, and totally attentive to your aids.

To get a circle with a diameter of 33 feet, measure in 17½ feet from the middle of a short side *or* a long side. Keep your eye on that point and describe a circle around it, staying one foot off the rail. For the time being I'll allow you to mark the center point somehow. Some people put a rock there, or a car hubcap, even a tire. But eventually you should know the location of that center point so well you won't need anything to show you where it is.

Tempting as the thought will probably be, don't draw an actual circle on the ground and ride over it. In order to see it you'll have to keep looking down at it, and that's not a good idea. You should look straight ahead of you or to the center of your circle at all times—but never down.

Your aids for a circle of this diameter are the same as for a larger one, except you'll be asking the horse for more of a bend. You maintain an even contact with both reins unless the horse resists or tries to evade your aids. You ask for the increased bend by directing the action of your outside wrist and forearm toward your inside hipbone (or toward the center of the circle). Your outside leg is behind the girth. Weight your inside seatbone slightly and look in to the center of the circle. Your inside leg also asks for the additional bend as well as for impulsion. Don't forget about that inside leg, because you won't get the horse bent to the circumference of the circle unless you use your inside leg correctly.

Your horse must move forward all the way around the circle without losing rhythm or impulsion and without resisting. If you notice that he seems to be hesitating and fighting the inside rein, it's probably because you haven't given his inside shoulder enough freedom. You're creating impulsion, and you mustn't restrict the forward movement of that inside shoulder by holding him back with your inside rein.

You *must* keep the horse going forward equally into both reins, and from now on it's going to be up to you to feel any problems of stiffness or evasion while you're working and to correct them when they happen. For instance, you might feel the horse's hindquarters just beginning to drift to the inside of the circle. A short, quick tap or two with your inside leg behind the girth will probably be enough to remind him to get his haunches over, or if he's beginning to stiffen his jaw against the bit you may have to combine your leg aid with a short squeeze on the stiff-sided rein. If he suddenly shoots his nose up in the air, you should know how to correct it. (If you don't, go back to the relevant information in Chapter 16 and memorize it.) Once you've corrected the problem, whatever it is, you arms, legs, hands, seat, etc., should all be in the regular balanced seat position. You should feel an even contact with the horse's mouth with both reins, and the horse should be moving straight forward.

A very good exercise to practice while you're working on circles is the spiral. Start with as big a circle as you can, at least 60 feet in diameter, and gradually make each successive circle smaller and smaller until you're on one that's 33–35 feet in diameter. (No smaller, though—your horse won't be able to do it correctly yet and there's no sense asking.) Decrease the size of your circles by using your outside rein against the horse's neck and your outside leg behind the girth to keep moving the horse's hindquarters in on the track of the spiral.

Once you've gotten down to your 33-foot circle, go out again, this time by decreasing the amount of bend. Move the horse into ever-widening circles by easing up slightly on your outside rein and directing it more and more toward your outside hip. Maintain constant pressure with your outside leg to make sure that the horse's hindquarters stay on the track. Use your inside leg slightly behind the girth to keep him moving outward. Watch his shoulder to make sure he doesn't lean in on the circle.

Now I'd like to introduce the full halt. You use exactly the same aids that you did for the half-halt; the only difference is that instead of using short, strong squeezes on the reins, you "hold" with your wrists and fingers until the horse is at a complete, four-square halt. As soon as he's halted, relax a little. For the half-halt you used the movement of your body to ask the horse to continue walking. For the halt, you relax.

A full-dress full halt. Otto Ammerman on Volturno (Germany) at the 3 Day World's Championships, Lexington, KY, 1978. (*Photo by Hillair Evans-Bell.*)

The horse has done what you wanted him to do, and he knows this is so because you relax: you're not asking him to do anything. But be sure to keep your legs on him even at the halt. You always want your horse to be thinking "forward."

Ask the horse to stand for a few minutes. He should be able to do this easily from his earlier work, and without fidgeting or trying to back or sidestep. When he's halted for the amount of time that you want, give him a pat on the neck and tell him he did well.

Through the contact with the bit you should have the sensation that he's eager to walk on again, that he *wants* to go forward. When you're ready, ask him to walk on again by bearing down with your seatbones and "asking" the horse's haunches. Pull your shoulder blades back and sit heavy in the saddle. As in the half-halt, the weight comes from your shoulders. Then resume your leg aids at the girth. As soon as the horse moves forward one step, praise him by stroking his neck with your inside hand and rein.

Remember those S-curves I had you doing down the length of the ring that I told you was a serpentine in three loops? Let's go back to the serpentine now and work on refining your aids.

First, draw your imaginary dollar-sign line down the center of the ring, parallel to the two long sides. (From now on I'll simply refer to it as the center line.) Begin at the posting trot on a half-circle to the right on the center line at one end of the ring. The diameter of each half-circle should be no smaller than 33 feet. As you make your first loop, the horse will be bent around your right leg. Your left leg is behind the girth and you're aiding with both legs together in the rhythm of the trot.

Maintain an even, firm contact with both reins. Your right seatbone is slightly weighted and your left shoulder is slightly in advance of your right one, the way the horse's is. The same "round" principle applies to serpentine loops that applies to circles. Mentally divide the ring into thirds and make sure that all three loops are round and *the same size.**

As you approach the center line, straighten your horse for

---

* In actual dressage competition, if you were to ride a serpentine in three loops, the loops would not be exact half-circles. But for the time being I'd like you to ride them as though they were.

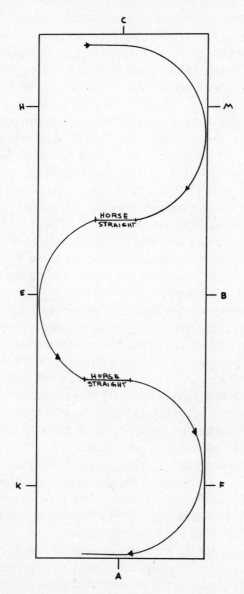

Serpentine in three loops.

one horse's length across the center line before asking him to bend to the left. To do this, you have to prepare him as his forehand *approaches* the center line. Begin transferring him from a bend to the right to a bend to the left so that for a couple of strides the horse is moving straight forward equally into both reins with a firm, elastic contact. Both your legs should be slightly behind the girth.

When your shoulders are directly above the center line, ask for the bend to the left. Weight your left seatbone slightly as you move your left leg up to the girth and aid simultaneously with your right leg behind the girth. You should be looking left, and the horse should be working into a steady, even rein contact, bending to the left.

Maintain the bend for the second half-circle, straighten your horse across the center line, and ask for the third and final half-circle by once again asking the horse for a bend to the right. When you reach the center line on the opposite rail, you've completed the movement.

As you practice making round serpentine loops, practice your transitions. Every time you approach the center line at a trot, come down to a walk for one horse's length as you cross it. Then pick up the trot again. Use half-halts for all these transitions. Or approach at the trot and halt the horse so that your shoulders are directly over the center line. Then ask him to trot on again. He should be able to do this easily if his hindquarters are engaged, and to move off into the trot immediately and without hesitation.

If you do a serpentine at the canter, be prepared to come down to a trot across the center line in order to change leads. Don't deliberately canter your horse on the wrong lead (called a "counter-canter"). This involves a higher degree of training than your horse has right now.

It will take you an enormous amount of practice to ride a serpentine correctly, especially when you begin to incorporate transitions across the center line. Remember that before you get too fancy you should have the basics well under control—the feeling that the horse is contained between your legs and hands, is moving freely forward with his inside shoulder, and is on the bit throughout the entire exercise.

Figure-8's are also very good suppling exercises. I've dealt with the correct way to ride a figure-8 in Chapter 14. Now you can ride smaller figure-8's, and concentrate on applying your aids with so much finesse that nobody will notice you doing it.

There are two main points to remember: one, ask your horse for the bend more subtly by sitting deeper into the saddle with your inside seatbone, by looking into the center of the circle so that your outside shoulder is slightly ahead of your inside shoulder, and by using your outside rein toward your inside hip. Two, a figure-8 has got a straight line at its center; use a half-halt to prepare your horse to go forward into both reins for a horse's length before you ask for the bend in the other direction. Make sure to maintain the same rhythm and tempo and the same forward movement throughout the whole figure. If you're careful never to let the impulsion slacken and never to ask roughly with your hands for the transitions, the horse won't hollow his back or come above the bit as you change direction through the straight line.

Now I'd like to introduce some lateral work.

All lateral movements involve working on two tracks: you deliberately position the horse so that his forehand is on one track and his hindquarters are on another. You'll find that lateral movements will improve your horse's responsiveness to the aids and will also help condition him because they allow his shoulders more freedom of movement than work on a single track, and will increase the "connectedness" between his jaw, poll, and hindquarters. Leg-yields, especially, are good for engaging the hindquarters and bending and strengthening the joints of the horse's hind leg. Leg-yields going to the left will help a horse that's stiff on that side, and

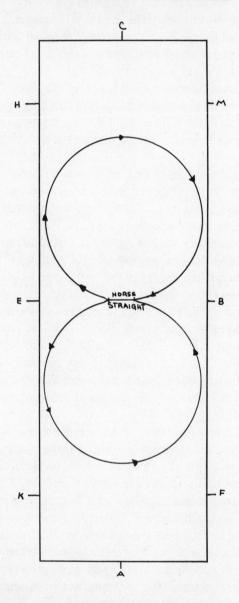

A figure eight. In a test the figure eight would be the width of the arena, beginning at E.

leg-yields going to the right will help overcome stiffness and resistance on the right side.

In most lateral movements (the exception is the one I'll be dealing with, the leg-yield), the horse is bent entirely around the rider's inside leg from poll to tail. Riders are often more concerned with the actual bend than with anything else, and they shouldn't be. Your main concern, always, should be with maintaining the rhythmic forward movement of the gait.

Leg-yielding is the most basic and easiest of all the lateral movements, and you should master it before you attempt any other work on two tracks. Leg-yields will teach your horse to move away from your leg—and that, simply stated, is what leg-yielding is. The horse will be moving forward and sideways at the same time, looking *away* from the direction he's moving in. (You will be looking *toward* the direction he's moving in.) The horse's body remains relatively straight, and by that I mean the bend is in his jaw and poll. All you should be able to see are the horse's inside eyelashes and his inside nostril. If you can see more of his face you're too concerned with the bend, and instead of a leg-yield you'll force the horse to bend his neck. Needless to say this isn't what you want. In the leg-yield you want the horse's forehand sufficiently in advance of his hindquarters that he crosses his inside legs in front of his outside legs. (In other words, if you're doing a leg-yield going to the left, the horse's right legs will cross in front of his left legs both in front and behind.)

I teach my students the leg-yield when they're going up the diagonal. It's easier for them to understand what I'm asking them to do and how it should look because they can use the straight long side of the ring to compare the angle of their horse's body to. Some trainers ask for it along the rail, but I find that it's more dificult to get the correct angle that way.

In the leg-yield you use lateral aids; that is, active aids on

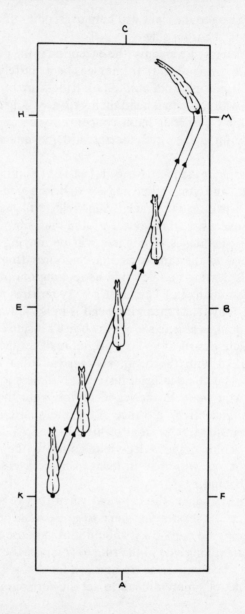

A leg-yield up the diagonal.

the same side (for instance, right rein and right leg). To begin with, I'd like you to ask for a leg-yield going to the left from a halt. As your horse is standing quietly at the halt, slightly increase the contact with your right rein in a light give-and-take. Move your right leg behind the girth and begin aiding in a walk rhythm. Nudge the horse's side until you actually push his hindquarters over to the left a step or two. Then ask him to walk on, patting his neck with your inside rein, and do it until you've done about half a circle.

(There is an exercise in dressage called a turn on the forehand. If you know it, don't mistake the explanation I just gave you for how to do a turn on the forehand, because the aids are incomplete. I use this approach to leg-yields in order to show my students how the horse responds to lateral aids.)

Ask for your first leg-yield from the walk. Start along the rail on the left rein. When you've passed the second corner of the short side, turn up the diagonal. When you ask for the leg-yield, the horse's spine will be parallel to the long side of the ring, although his forehand will be slightly in advance of his hindquarters—his forehand will get to the opposite rail before his hindquarters will.

At this point it will probably begin to dawn on you that what I'm calling a leg-yield is very similar to the first little exercise I asked you to do in "Turns and Corners."

As you walk up the diagonal, move your right leg back a little behind the girth. You'll be using your right rein in a give-and-take toward your left hip so that the horse's head remains positioned slightly to the right. (In the beginning stages you'll probably be doing a little more holding than giving.) You'll be using your right leg in unison with the horse's right leg: every time the horse starts to put his right leg down, push it sideways, to the left, so that it crosses in front of his left hind leg.

If you don't use the rhythm of the walk to push his right hind leg over, you're not going to get this exercise at all. In-

stead of allowing the horse to put his right hind leg down in the track of his right front leg—as he would do if he were tracking straight—you're asking him to put it down behind his *left* front leg.

Be careful that the horse doesn't bend his neck too much. You must keep an even contact with both reins so that the horse continues to move forward into your hands and doesn't simply move sideways and bend his neck too far to the right. Your outside leg, which remains at the girth, also aids in keeping the horse moving forward.

Hilda Gurney on Good Evening performing a leg-yield to the right. The horse's forehand is advancing before his hindquarters, and the horse's body is bent around the rider's inside leg. (*Photos by Hillair Evans-Bell.*)

When you reach the opposite corner, go away along the rail to your right in a trot or canter. Go through the first corner and the second corner, and come down to a walk again in preparation for a leg-yield to the right. Turn down the opposite diagonal, and use the opposite aids.

Don't practice any lateral movement for more than a few minutes at a time. The horse must be moving slightly sideways all the time and this is tiring for him, especially if

Kathy Reinecke on Annex at a first-level working trot. Compare the horse's overall muscle development, but especially the rounding of the hindquarters, with Keen's in the following photo. (*Photo by Hillair Evans-Bell.*)

you're too concerned with the amount of bend. Always follow any lateral work immediately with work on a single track at an energetic trot or canter, so the horse can move straight forward.

You'll undoubtedly find that your horse will go to a leg-yield more easily on one side than on the other. Practice going to the side he needs work on, not the side he goes best to.

Hilda Gurney on Keen performing the piaffe. The piaffe is the culmination of years of hard training—a trot in place with only slight forward movement and a longer moment of suspension. But the horse is still thinking *forward*. Hilda and Keen were members of the USET for the 1976 Olympics in Montreal when the squad won a bronze medal. (*Photo by Hillair Evans-Bell.*)

Most of my students try to make more out of this movement than necessary. Leg-yielding is a very simple and basic movement, and you don't have to contort either your body or your horse's body into a pretzel. Don't be overly concerned with getting the horse to move sideways. The first few tries he'll probably move sideways just a couple of steps and then refuse to do any more, because he's not sure what you want. If that happens, trot him straight on for a few strides and then come back down to a walk and try it again. Sometimes using your whip will help, if your horse doesn't understand what you're asking for—or understands but prefers not to do it. Every time that you nudge with your leg behind the girth, tap him with the whip behind your leg.

Once you've mastered the leg-yield at the walk and have a

free forward movement, try it at the sitting trot. Don't try it at the canter. At this level it's too difficult, simply because of the sequence of legs involved (all six of them—yours and the horse's).

Practice circles—and make sure they're round. Practice corners at the walk, the trot, and the canter, with half-halts. Then practice leg-yields for a few more minutes. Then work on something else.

Whether you realize it or not you have a lot of "something elses" to choose from. You and your horse have both come a long way from your first tentative journey along the rail at a walk, turning from an open rein position and telling yourself sternly, "Eyes ahead, chin in, heels down, *relax . . .*" You have balance, confidence, and a beautifully attentive horse that goes willingly forward in whatever gait or exercise you ask for.

Do you know what else you have? A horse that's ready to show off in a formal dressage competition.

Part Five
THE COMPLETE
PLEASURE HORSE

18
Riding in Competition

In a dressage competition, unlike other types of horse shows, you compete against yourself. You and your horse perform specific movements in a ring by yourselves. A judge scores each movement of your ride, and you get the test paper back after the competition to find out how you did.* All horses and riders at the same level of proficiency ride the same test. For instance, you, as a beginner, would ride Training Level, Test 1, and so would all the other riders who have never ridden in a dressage competition.

The movements required in all three Training Level tests are ones you already know: going along the rail, corners, and circles at the three gaits, with transitions between gaits and a full halt. After that, things get harder, although all of the 17 tests include at least one of the movements I've taught you in this book. The tests range in difficulty from Training Level to Grand Prix, which asks for movements such as the passage, the piaffer, half and full pirouettes, and a change of lead at every stride for 15 strides. Grand Prix dressage is Olympic-level dressage, and for the serious competitor it's the ultimate in dedication and achievement. The rest of us would just as soon ride in a dressage show every once in a while. Most of my students look forward to competing— they enjoy getting together with other riders, and they find

* A copy of an actual dressage test appears later in this chapter.

the whole aura of competitive show riding very exciting.

If you do decide to compete, you should probably get a trainer. You can't learn everything from a book, even this book.

You should also get yourself a regulation dressage ring. You can make one within an existing arena very easily, by laying down enough 2×4 boards to make a rectangular ring that's 20 meters by 60 meters, or 66 feet by 198 feet. (Beginning level tests are often given in a small arena that's 20 meters by 40 meters, or 66 feet by 132 feet. But if you have the room, make a large arena.) You'll also need to put up dressage letters, which you can paint or draw on pieces of cardboard. Nobody knows how this particular series of letters evolved, but it's always been used and probably always will be.

You should also join your local dressage organization. Besides giving you information on upcoming shows and clinics, most organizations will also provide you with copies of current tests. To find out the address of the dressage association in your area, write to:

The United States Dressage Federation
Box 80668
Lincoln, NE 68501

The purpose of each dressage test, the method of scoring, the conditions (required tack, time limit, etc.) and the penalties are all printed on every test. The judge will score you on whether the horse performs what's written on the test—the correct movement, in the correct gait, at the correct time (i.e., at the correct letter). Each movement is numbered (the test in this chapter has eleven movements), and after each one is a directive which explains what the judge will be looking for. Is the halt square and absolutely immobile? Is the horse bending to the circumference of the circle? Is the circle round?

After the directives there's space for your score. The judge

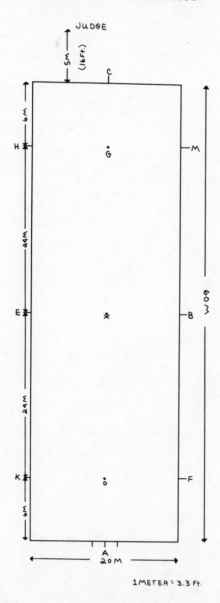

1 METER = 3.3 Ft.

A large dressage arena, 20 meters by 60 meters, or 66 feet by 198 feet. (1 meter = 3.3 feet.)

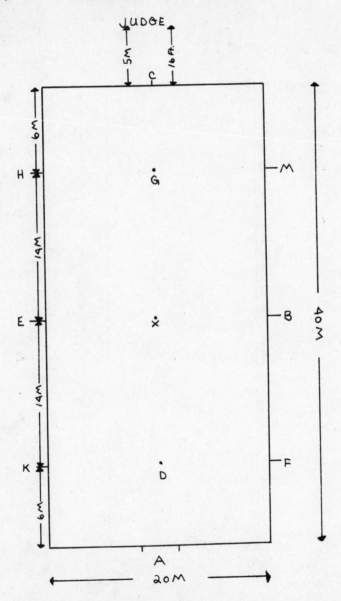

A small dressage arena, 20 meters by 40 meters, or 66 feet by 132 feet.

will score each movement of the test from zero to 10. Zero means that you didn't do the movement or that you or your horse fell, while 10 is absolute and flawless perfection. Judges seldom if ever give 10's and rarely give 9's, so for all practical purposes your score will range between 0 and 8. If you get a 5 or lower, there's room for improvement. If you get a 6 or 7, you're doing all right. I advise my students to get a score of 60% or higher on three different rides for three different judges before moving up to the next test. (For a beginner, the next test would be Training Level, Test 2.) If you want to introduce your horse to a higher level of competition, you are permitted to compete in two consecutive levels at the same show. For instance, you can show at Training Level, Tests 1 and 3, or Training Level, Test 3 and First Level, Test 1. You're not allowed to skip a *level,* but you can skip a test.

There is also a space on your test for remarks. Typical judges' remarks are: "Weaving on the center line." "Not straight." "Transition rough." "Lacking impulsion." "Obvious aids." "Behind the bit" (or "behind the vertical"). "Rhythm uneven." "Cutting corners." "Circle irregular." Here is where you'll find out whether you did a rising trot when you were supposed to be doing a sitting trot, or whether you were posting on the wrong diagonal.

At the bottom of the test is a section headed Collective Marks, where the judge will evaluate your overall performance (again on a score of 0 to 10). The horse is rated on the freedom and regularity of his gaits and his willingness to move forward in a relaxed manner. The rider is scored on his seat, his position in the saddle, and the correctness of his aids.

What I look for as a judge in a beginning horse and rider is whether the horse goes willingly straight forward in a relaxed, even rhythm without resisting. Resistance is especially noticeable during transitions, when the rider's hands have the greatest effect, and I particularly watch to see that the transitions are smooth and seemingly effortless on the part of both horse and rider.

I want to see a horse flexing properly, at the poll, and not at the second or third vertebra because the rider has tried to "set" his head.

I tend to stress the total picture of the horse's performance rather than the correctness of individual movements. Does the horse accept a light contact with the bit? Does he look relaxed and happy?

As far as the rider is concerned, I watch mainly to see what the rider asks the horse to do. Does he or she ask the horse to bend or straighten according to the track they're on, or does he allow the horse to evade? Are his aids light and unobtrusive? Does he look as though he's having a relaxed, comfortable, enjoyable ride? As with the horse, I stress the total picture—one of ease, harmony, and fluidity.

Suppose you've definitely decided to compete. You've joined your local dressage association, received copies of the current AHSA tests, and picked out the competition you and your horse are going to debut in. What do you do next?

The first thing you do is memorize your test. In most cases you can have somebody read your test out loud to you while you're actually in the ring. But I've found that my rides go much more smoothly if I'm able to concentrate on *how* the horse is going instead of *where* the horse is going.

It's easy to learn a test by heart. The trick is to not let your horse learn the test by heart. The method that I'm going to explain works very well for me, although other people have other methods.

Read completely through your test a few times until you have a general idea of what's in it. Then mark out a mini dressage ring, with letters, someplace in your house or yard. You'll probably have noticed that there's a pattern to the test: each series of movements is performed first in one direction of the ring and then in the opposite direction. For instance, movement number 2 reads, "C, track to the right;

M, working trot (rising); B, circle width of the arena."
(Translation: you've entered at A and are going down the
center line of the arena. At C turn right, along the rail. Ride
through your corner and at M ask for a working trot. Continue along the rail to B at the rising trot, and when you
reach B make a circle the width of the arena, i.e., a circle
with a diameter of 66 feet or 20 meters.) Movement number
4 asks for the same sequence of movements except you track
left at C.

Go completely through the test, one movement at a time,
by walking it or crawling it on your hands and knees. As you
go through each movement think about what you and your
horse should be doing. How do you ask for the turn to the
right at C? (The way you would for any other corner.) How
do you ride through the corner and ask for the working trot
at M? (Carefully.)

Go through the entire test a time or two. Then try to isolate any problems your horse has, things you're going to
have to watch out for. Then go ride your horse.

As you ride through the test, make sure that you ride
through the movements in a different order than the one
they're given in. Your horse is much quicker at learning
patterns than you are and will memorize the test for you if
you're not careful. This isn't a good idea, because he'll anticipate upcoming movements by himself instead of waiting for
you to tell him what you want. If he knows he's supposed to
canter at K, he'll more than likely anticipate it halfway there
and break into a canter without being asked. You'll bring
him down, he'll get agitated, and instead of doing a relaxed
working trot to K, he'll jig and wring his tail and in general
ignore you because he *knows* he's supposed to canter at K.

Work on any movement or set of movements that he has
trouble with, but not to the exclusion of everything else on
the test. If you find you can't remember the order of the
movements, go back to your living room on your hands and
knees. You want to know this test backward and forward

and inside out—you want to sleep, eat, and dream this test, and if you're going to dream it, you might as well dream it right.

The second thing you do is make sure that you know all of the AHSA rules for dressage competition.

The third thing you do is make sure you're prepared. You've probably realized by now that you can't compete in your trail riding outfit of jeans and a cowboy hat. Your dress has to conform to AHSA regulations, which specify that you must wear either a hunt cap or a derby. You must have white or light tan breeches and plain black riding boots, preferably leather, that come to the knee. A white hunt shirt with a stock tie and gold pin is also required, to be worn with a black or dark-colored hunting coat. Your coat should be a solid color; no plaids, checks, or stripes. I prefer to see beginners ride in black gloves, either cloth or leather, that don't call attention to their hands. But if you feel that your hands don't move very much, you're permitted to wear white or tan.

Your very first dressage competition is no place to try on all your brand new clothes for the first time. If you had to go out and buy a hunt coat and derby, wear them around the house and ride in them for a while until you're used to them. And don't sacrifice your comfort for some eye-catching outfit. You want to look *and* feel good on your horse.

Women should make plans to secure their hair with bobby pins, hair spray, or a hairnet—whatever will keep it under your hat and out of your face. If you wear makeup, keep it simple.

Now isn't the time to buy fancy new tack for your horse either. Your horse isn't going to Hollywood. What you're required to compete in is what you've been using all along—an English saddle, a plain leather headstall with a regular cavesson or a dropped noseband, and a snaffle bit. I do suggest that you get your horse a white string girth to show in, just because they look nice. I'd also suggest that you take an extra girth and an extra set of reins with you to the show grounds. Side reins, running reins, and martingales of any kind are not permitted in the ring, and a horse can't wear boots or bandages into the ring. As I've said before, your horse's conformation per se will not count for him or against him. But if it affects his way of going badly enough so he's visibly lame, he'll be disqualified.

The day of the show you should have your horse as shiny and clean as you can get him—hoofs, nostrils, dock, ears, eyes, tail. I wouldn't advise you to try to keep him that way by using any of the commercial preparations designed to highlight a horse's coat, because after your horse has worked for a while his coat will pick up dust and get very greasy-looking.

Be sure to take a smock or dust coat with you to the show grounds to wear over your clothes. It's a help to take a friend or two along too. You can give one of them a brush to remove any last-minute specks of dust from your horse, and another a clean cloth to give your boots a final swipe as you head for the ring. And it's very nice for the ego to have your own cheering section.

Also take a grooming kit for last-minute touch-ups, and a sponge—so that you horse's white legs are still white when he goes into the ring.

Here's a hint for getting an especially flowing, full tail for a show. Instead of combing it, which will break the hairs, give yourself about half an hour and separate the entire tail, hair by hair, with your fingers.

You should braid your horse's mane—it makes for a very neat appearance and it also shows off your horse's conformation. Be sure the mane is short and that you've thinned and pulled it. There are numerous books and articles available on how to braid a mane so I won't go into it here. I do suggest that you wrap each braid with eighth- or quarter-inch white adhesive tape. It keeps the braids from coming down and it makes for a very showy appearance.

Temporary dressing room. (*Photo by Joan Fry.*)

Make sure that your dress is clean, your tack is clean, you're clean. Don't ride with spots on your breeches and mud all over your boots. You want to look as shined-up and tidy and *prepared* as you possibly can. Your attitude will be a reflection on the show and the people in it, and they'll appreciate it. It will also tell the judge that you're trying to look your best, and that you expect to be taken seriously.

You'll be notified before the day of the show what time you're scheduled to ride. But sometimes horse shows don't run as planned, and you might be asked to ride earlier. You don't have to though—you can say you'd rather wait and ride at your scheduled time.

Try to arrive at the show grounds at least two hours in advance. Even the most mild-mannered horse will probably get excited in unfamiliar surroundings, with dogs and people and strange horses milling around. So don't pull in at the last minute, throw the saddle on, and expect your horse to go calmly into his warm-up exercises.

Do pack your lunging equipment. Lunging will get him

This horse is calmly surveying the goings-on around him. (*Photo by Joan Fry.*)

warmed up while it takes the edge off him, and you won't have to worry about his embarrassing you by bucking you off in front of all those people. (And often the warm-up ring will be too crowded to work in anyway.) Then tack him up and go for a sight-seeing tour. Ride your horse all over the show grounds. Let him look at the horse trailers, the judges' stands (they will be set up at the end of the dressage arena at C), the flowers, the concession stands. Some judges' stands are shaded by umbrellas. Let your horse go up to them and get a good look at them and if possible take a sniff of them, so he knows what they are and won't shy at them in the middle of your test.

Even Hilda Gurney and Keen need to get warmed up. (*Photo by Joan Fry.*)

Then warm your horse up. It should only take you half an hour, at most, until your horse is relaxed and going forward with impulsion to the bit, and working well under you. Now is not the time to try to cram a month's worth of work into one 20-minute warm-up session. If your horse doesn't know the test by now, this is no time to start teaching him.

When you read over the test you probably noticed that it didn't say anything about the horse being on the bit. The main thing all three Training Level tests look for is a relaxed horse that is willing to go straight forward *to* the bit and accept the rider's hands. In other words, the horse must be moving forward with enough impulsion to reach for a contact with the bit. But if your horse is already on the bit, so much the better.

Each test tells you how long it should take you to complete it. Training Level tests have no time limit; you have five minutes in the small arena and six minutes in the large arena to complete First Level, Test 1. Don't be afraid you have to rush to finish in time. The times are given solely as a guideline—how long the average rider, riding at this level, will take to complete this test. If your horse does his gaits at a normal rate of speed and you execute all the movements correctly, you'll finish in plenty of time.

If you make a mistake—let the horse take the wrong lead, or suddenly realize you're posting on the wrong diagonal—correct yourself *immediately*. Change diagonals. Bring the horse back down to a trot and ask him for the correct lead, even if you have to do it two or three times before he gets it right. It's better than allowing him to keep cantering on the wrong lead, because then the judge will think you don't know any better.

If you make a mistake off course—for instance, if you track left instead of right at C—the judge will ring a bell to let you know you're wrong. He'll mark the error on your test and then tell you verbally where you went wrong and where to take up the test again.

If your horse leaves the ring before the test is over so that all four feet are outside of the ring, you'll be eliminated.

You're not allowed to use a dressage whip during a test unless you're riding sidesaddle. (And if you are, you didn't learn it from me.) If you use a whip while you're warming up, remember to drop it before you enter the ring. I haven't talked very much about spurs because they're often misused by beginning riders who don't realize how easy it is to deaden a horse's sides with them. But if your horse is lazy enough to need the whip constantly throughout training, you'll be better off in the long run with the Prince of Wales spurs I mentioned in Part One. Spurs are permissible in a dressage test.

Using your voice, however, is not permissible. Every time the judge hears you clucking or talking to your horse or to yourself, you will be penalized two points.

When it's your turn to ride your test, the judge will ring a bell. If you don't enter the ring and begin your ride within one minute, you'll be disqualified.

In order to show you how to ride a dressage test correctly I'm going to take you through the 1976 Training Level, Test 3 step by step. Although this particular test is no longer used, Test 3 is the most difficult of the Training Level tests and if you can do this one you can do the other two.*

As a judge, this is the way I'd like to see a horse and rider do this test.

The bell has rung and you're still outside the ring. Ask your horse for a working trot and approach A so that the dressage ring is on your left. Just past A make a 10-meter circle to the right (outside of the ring). You know that you have to enter at a sitting trot, that you have to go from A to C, and that at C you have to turn to the right. So before you even enter the ring, make a circle to the right to get your horse bending. When you ask him to track to the right at C, he'll give you an even, rounded corner.

When you reach A again, come in off your circle and enter the ring on a straight line. Your legs should be slightly behind the girth so that you have control of the horse's hindquarters. You want to make sure they don't drift off to the side. All the judge should see is your horse's neck, head, and chest, and you, head-on.

In the middle of the ring, between E and B, is an imaginary letter, X. Continue down the center line at an even, re-

---

* The AHSA dressage committee re-evaluates the tests periodically, and it's always wise to check and see whether the test you're using is still current.

1976 Training Level Test 3

	TEST	DIRECTIVE IDEAS	POINTS	CO-EFFICIENT	TOTAL	REMARKS
1 A X G	ENTER WORKING TROTS (SITTING) MEDIUM WALK HALT, SALUTE PROCEED, MEDIUM WALK	STRAIGHTNESS, TRANSITIONS IMMOBILITY, MOVE OFF FROM WALK				
2 C M B	TRACK TO THE RIGHT WORKING TROT (RISING) CIRCLE WIDTH OF THE ARENA	REGULARITY, SHAPE OF THE CIRCLE, FLEXION OF THE HORSE				
3 B-A A	WORKING TROT (RISING) TURN DOWN CENTER LINE WORKING TROT (SITTING)	REGULARITY AND STRAIGHTNESS				
4 C H E	TRACK TO THE LEFT WORKING TROT (RISING) CIRCLE WIDTH OF THE ARENA	REGULARITY, SHAPE OF THE CIRCLE, FLEXION OF THE HORSE				
5 E-K K-A B	WORKING TROT (SITTING) WORKING CANTER LEFT LEAD CIRCLE WIDTH OF THE ARENA	CALMNESS AND SMOOTHNESS OF THE DEPART, SHAPE OF THE CIRCLE, FLEXION OF THE HORSE				
6 B H	WORKING TROT (SITTING) MEDIUM WALK	TRANSITIONS AND REGULARITY				
7 E X B	TURN LEFT WORKING TROT (SITTING) TURN RIGHT	CALMNESS AND SMOOTHNESS OF THE DEPART, SHAPE OF THE CIRCLE, FLEXION OF THE HORSE				
8 F-A E	WORKING CANTER RIGHT LEAD CIRCLE WIDTH OF THE ARENA	TRANSITIONS AND REGULARITY				
9 E C	WORKING TROT (SITTING) MEDIUM WALK	TRANSITIONS AND REGULARITY				

10 M-E K	CHANGE REIN WORKING TROT (SITTING)	REGULARITY OF THE WALK THE TRANSITION		
11 A X G	TURN DOWN CENTER LINE MEDIUM WALK HALT, SALUTE LEAVE ARENA. FREE WALK ON A LOOSE REIN	STRAIGHTNESS, TRANSITIONS IMMOBILITY, RELAXATION AT THE FREE WALK		

COLLECTIVE MARKS:

GAITS (FREEDOM AND REGULARITY)	2	
WILLINGNESS TO MOVE FORWARD, CONTACT AND RELAXATION	2	
POSITION, SEAT OF THE RIDER, CORRECT USE OF AIDS	2	

SUBTOTAL _____

ERRORS (−   )

TOTAL POINTS _____

laxed trot. Without turning your head, glance over at either E or B. When you've gotten halfway to X prepare your horse for the walk by asking for a half-halt. As your shoulders reach X ask for the walk* and begin to use your legs alternately to make sure the horse maintains impulsion.

G is another imaginary letter on the center line, this one between H and M. Halfway between X and G, half-halt your horse to prepare him for the full halt at G. Then very quietly ask for the halt by closing your shoulder blades, bracing your back, sitting down into the saddle, closing your legs around the horse, and closing your fingers.

When your horse has halted, salute the judge. If you're a man, transfer the reins to your left hand. With your right hand remove your hat, then drop your arm to your side, hat in hand. Don't show the lining of the hat to the judge; he's not interested in where your hat was made. Bow your head. When the judge acknowledges your salute, return the hat to your head and take up the reins in both hands and proceed with the test. If you're a woman rider, transfer the reins to your left hand and drop your right hand to your side so that your arm is straight, knuckles forward. Nod your head. Then look up, smiling, and wait until the judge acknowledges your salute. Then resume your ride.

Remember: you're allowed to breathe.

Ask for the walk by bearing down with your seatbones and closing your legs in short actions against the horse's sides. Continue straight toward the end of the ring. About one horse's length before C begin preparing your horse for the turn to the right. Close your inside leg at the girth, sit down deep on your inside seatbone, and move your outside leg back to guide the horse's hindquarters around your turn. Contact should be even in both reins. You ask for the bend

---

* None of the 1979 Training Level tests ask for a medium walk. If you're practicing this test at home, ask your horse for an ordinary working walk.

Hilda Gurney on Keen—a perfect four-square halt. The rider salutes the judge at the beginning and end of every test. (*Photo by Hillair Evans-Bell.*)

with your seatbone and by turning your shoulders from the hips. Make sure the horse doesn't bend his neck too far to the inside by using your outside rein.

Now you immediately have a corner coming up. Use the same aids that you used for the turn at C.

About half a horse's length before you get to M, half-halt your horse to prepare for the transition into the trot. Remember to stay about a foot off the rail. As your shoulders pass M, ask for the trot with short, quick squeezes of your legs.

Pay special attention to where the horse's hindquarters are, because you're going away from the judge and that's what he can see best—the horse's hindquarters. Make sure that his haunches are aligned with his forehand and that the horse is *straight*. And since you're doing the rising trot, also make sure that you're on the left diagonal.

As you approach B, come very slightly off the rail. The instant your shoulders pass B, look in to the center of your circle, which is X. Don't just turn your head and neck; turn from your hips. Keep your eyes on X and stay the same distance away from it all the way around your circle, maintaining an even contact with both reins all the way to E. Your outside rein should be directed toward your inside seatbone. As you approach E you will be coming in to the rail on a perfect half-circle. Continue on past E, your inside leg at the girth, your outside leg behind the girth to keep the horse bent to the circumference of the circle. (If the horse still tends to let his haunches fall into the circle, you'll have to reverse your leg aids until he tracks straight.)

When you return to B, come off your circle and straighten the horse.

Continue straight along the rail. Then prepare for your next bend coming up at the corner.

Ride through your corner as though it were exactly a quarter of a circle. At A you have to turn down the center line at the sitting trot, so about two horse's lengths before A, sit down to the trot. Then, about one horse's length before A, ask your horse for a bend to the right.

Then straighten your horse down the center line. Move both legs back slightly behind the girth and continue the sitting trot straight down the center line, looking at the judge and *smiling*.

Show that you're glad to be here and that you're not the least bit nervous about showing in front of this judge.

You're proud of your horse and pleased with his performance.

At G, the imaginary letter between H and M, prepare for
the corner that's coming up at C where you track to the left.

Change reins smoothly at C. You now have another corner, another quarter-circle, coming up.

When your shoulders reach H, begin rising on the right
diagonal. Continue along the rail at the rising trot, aiding
simultaneously with both legs so the horse can feel the
rhythm of the gait from the movements of your body.

At E you have another 20-meter circle. Bring the horse
slightly off the rail before you reach E. As your shoulders
approach E, locate X. Keep exactly that far away from X
until you've done a perfect half-circle and have reached the
rail at B. Then continue your other half-circle around X
back to E, your departure point.

As you reach E, straighten your horse and sit to the trot,
again making sure the horse's hindquarters are in line with
the forehand. (I'm stressing this point so strongly because a
lot of riders forget the horse has a back half when they're
riding a test.) You have to prepare for two things: for the
canter on the left lead between K and A, and for the upcoming corner. The test gives you a little leeway on this
movement. Show the judge that you can strike off on the
canter at K. Since you'll be asking for the bend at that corner, ask for the canter at the same time. The horse should
pick up the correct lead.

So: as you approach K, half-halt your horse and ask for
the canter. Go through the first corner. Go past A through
the second corner. Your corners should be round and even.
Don't let the horse speed up; be careful to maintain the same
even rhythm.

At B you have another circle the width of the arena. Keep
your eye on X and make sure your horse doesn't try to lean
in on his inside shoulder and that the rhythm remains
steady. Keep the same even contact with both reins all the

way around the circle unless you need to half-halt the horse to keep him balanced on his haunches.

About two horse's lengths before you get back to B, half-halt your horse, and when your shoulders pass B ask for the sitting trot.

Continue past M, go through the corner and past C. As you go through the second corner, half-halt, and at H ask for the walk. The horse should be relaxed, and his strides should be even and regular.

Prepare the horse for your turn at E. Between E and X ask for the half-halt, and ask for the sitting trot as you cross the center line at X.

At B you're going to track to the right, so halfway between X and B ask the horse to bend slightly to the right to prepare for the corner.

When you reach the rail, continue down the long side.

As you approach F, you'll have to prepare for two things: the upcoming corner and the canter. Take advantage of the fact that the horse must be bending correctly in order to go through the corner. At F ask him for a half-halt, and as you go into the corner ask him for a canter on the right lead. Continue on past A, around the second corner, and along the rail.

At E, circle the width of the arena the way you did before, by keeping your eye on X. Make sure the horse remains bent to the circumference of the circle.

About four or five horse's lengths before you return to E, half-halt to prepare for the working trot. When your shoulders are directly above E, ask for the trot and sit down to it.

Continue past H, and as you go around the corner prepare the horse with a half-halt and at C ask for the walk. Make sure that the transition is as smooth as you can make it so the horse doesn't hollow his back or come above the bit, and that the walk is a cadenced, four-beat walk. The horse won't resist if you've prepared him through the half-halt. Continue around the corner and about a horse's length past it, prepare to leave the rail at M. Turn up the diagonal.* Your horse should be looking and bending slightly to the right.

As you cross the center line, straighten your horse for one horse's length and then ask for a slight bend to the left. You're preparing the horse for the turn at the rail to E so he'll do it roundly and smoothly. Plan to reach the opposite long side about one horse's length before E, so that by the time your shoulder is at E the horse is absolutely parallel to the long side.

Halfway between E and K prepare for the sitting trot by a half-halt, and when your shoulders are over the letter, ask the horse for a working trot. Be sure to continue asking for impulsion and make sure the horse is going forward to the bit so that you can make a clean, nicely-rounded corner.

You're going to have to turn down the center line at A, so approximately one horse's length before you reach A, ask the horse for another corner, and turn to the left.

Ride straight up the center line with your legs slightly behind the girth. Halfway between A and X half-halt your horse and at X ask him for the walk. Continue straight forward. Halfway between X and G prepare for the full halt by asking for a half-halt. Close your legs around his sides, close your shoulders, sit down in the saddle and close your fingers around the reins. The horse will halt.

Salute the judge the same way you did at the beginning of your test. When the judge returns your salute, you may leave the arena the way you came in, at A.

The test reads, "Halt, salute, leave arena, **free walk** on a loose rein." Although the test doesn't tell you how to leave the arena, this is the way I like to see it done.

When the judge has returned your salute, loosen the reins

---

* Although this movement is a method of changing rein, a true "change of rein through the diagonal" would take you through the center of the ring—MXK OR FXH. The 1979 Training Level, Test 3 asks for a change of rein through the diagonal.

by letting the horse stretch forward so that the reins slide through your fingers. Continue up the center line toward C, and make sure that the horse is still overstepping the tracks of his forehand. A free walk is a good, active walk.

When you reach C, track right. Do a round corner and ride straight down the long side. Ride through the first short corner—and then continue on past A. Although a lot of riders leave the ring at this point, the judge may still be watching you, trying to decide whether a particular movement deserved a 5, a 6, or a 7—and a little finesse may alter his mark in your favor. Continue around the corner, past K, and halfway between K and E make a half-circle back to the center line. Come off your half-circle on the center line and go straight out at A.

Your test is now finished.

Untack your horse, cool him out, water him and make sure he's comfortable. Then you can go and find out how you did on your test.

Let's say you received a score of 72%. If that mark was higher than the mark for any other Training Level, Test 3 ride, you and your horse took top honors. But let's say you got a considerably lower score; what do you do about it?

Go talk to the judge—not, let me stress, in order to complain, but to find out what you did wrong and how you can improve your horse. Judges have to work quickly when they're scoring a test and will often put down standardized comments, like "lacks impulsion," which cover a variety of ills and probably won't help you too much. If you ask the judge what he meant by that, and why he marked the movement the way he did, he'll be only too glad to give you a complete explanation. Don't forget that judges are also horsemen and competitors themselves. A good judge should teach you as well as tell you what you did wrong.

Then go home and go over your entire test. Be as critical of your ride as the judge was. "Circle irregular": were you trying to do a bigger circle than the one required because

An excellent extended trot at the Grand Prix level—Inez Propfé-Credo on Marius. Inez and Marius competed in Mexico in 1968 with the Canadian Olympic Dressage Team.

your horse can't quite do one that size yet? If that's the case, you have no business riding that particular test.

Work with your horse on the movements and transitions that gave you trouble. When you think you've got the problem licked, ride the test for another judge. I guarantee you'll get a better score.

Remember that in dressage you compete against yourself. If you make excuses for your performance and pout and carry on about your low score, you're not doing yourself any favors. You're only depriving yourself of the enjoyment of a unique, exciting sport in which you can compete on equal footing with the best the world has to offer.

19
Riding for Pleasure

It's a beautiful day. The sky is a flawless blue, the sun is shining, and the ground is soft and springy underfoot. You've been planning on doing a little more work on leg-yields today, but as you walk to the barn where your horse is stabled, you think, "I'd rather go for a ride."

So you groom your horse, clean his feet, saddle and bridle him, and you're ready to go. But first you want to lunge him. He follows you obediently and with anticipation to the ring, because he's looking forward to what's coming next. You close the gate and let him go. He's so glad to be alive that he's a joy to watch. When he runs out of steam he stops and waits while you attach the lunge line and lunge him a few minutes. Then you undo the throatlatch, uncross the bridle reins, and fasten the throatlatch again. The buckle's a little stiff, and it takes you a minute, but your horse stands quietly, without fussing. You put your foot in the stirrup iron and swing over his back. He doesn't move a muscle. When you're settled in the saddle you ask him to "walk on"—and you're on your way.

You're looking forward to this ride. Your horse feels good too, and moves forward to the bit with long, elastic strides, alert and attentive.

Why not canter? you think.

Why not indeed?

So you ask for a trot first, so your horse can balance himself. He doesn't fight you to go faster; your contact with his mouth remains light and steady, even though you know he wants to canter too. Then you ask for a canter on the right lead, since you know that the trail ahead goes off to the right. Because you've prepared him, your horse moves smoothly from a balanced, rhythmical trot into a balanced, rhythmical canter. The aids you gave him were so slight he almost seemed to have read your mind. And you feel a surge of exhilaration in your heart. The canter is so effortless, so free, that the two of you almost seem to be moving as one being, floating effortlessly over the field in a sea of grass.

There's the trail—you were enjoying yourself so much you almost missed it. You ask your horse for the turn and he does it without effort or resistance. You can feel him bending throughout his whole body, and when he straightens, you bring him down to a quiet walk and pat his neck.

The trail is shady even in summer, cathedral-like with flashes of sunlight through the leaves. Your horse walks calmly, one ear back toward you and the other on the trail ahead. You can feel everything else begin to slip away from you—frustrations with your job, the stress of daily living— and you heave a sigh of contentment.

Suddenly there's a loud whirring noise almost under your feet. Your horse swivels both ears around and looks intently, but continues forward without missing a stride. You're not quite as self-possessed. What was *that,* you wonder—as a grouse bursts through the underbrush just ahead of you.

Your horse takes absolutely no notice whatsoever.

Well, well, you muse. A grouse. One of nature's small miracles, like squirrels and horses and human patience. You give your horse another appreciative pat and continue on your way. The trail forks later on, you remember. One way passes by an old tumbled-down farmhouse, and the other . . . Come to think of it, you've never taken that other trail. Where *does* it go? Today's a good day to find out. Your horse is relaxed and feeling good and confident of you, and you're on top of the world.

(*Photo by John Havey.*)

And that's as it should be in dressage. It *was* a long road, but it was worth it. No longer does your horse shy and evade your hands and try to get his own way. He responds eagerly to whatever you ask for, and his movements are so easy and cadenced and he looks so elegant that people at the stable—who have known him for years—have been whispering, "Who's *that?*"

You tell them "That's my dressage horse."

Glossary

Above the bit. The horse is resisting the rider's hands by poking his nose out. His face is in front of the vertical, his back is hollow, and his hocks are out behind him. (Also see *on the bit.*)

Aids. The means by which the rider communicates with his horse. There are two types of aids. Natural aids include the voice, legs, arms, hands, back, seat, shoulders, and weight. Artificial aids include the bit, reins, whip, and spurs.

Balance. A horse is naturally balanced, as you can see by watching one play in a field, but a rider adds weight to the horse's forehand. By using his seat and other aids, the rider must ask the horse to move his hind legs farther under his body so that he's balanced again and carries the rider's weight rather than pushing it. A horse can be balanced without being collected, but he can't be collected without being balanced.

Behind the bit. The horse is resisting the rider's hands by tucking his nose into his chest and dropping the contact with the bit. (Also see *on the bit.*)

Cadence. Energy and springiness of stride. Natural elevation resulting from the strengthening of the stifle, hock, and fetlock joints through increased impulsion.

Canter. One of the horse's natural gaits. The canter has three beats followed by a moment of suspension. For a canter on the right lead the sequence of legs is: left hind, one beat; right hind and left fore simultaneously, second beat; right fore, third beat. A horse should be able to complete approximately 40 strides per minute at the working canter.

Change of rein. Change of direction. The rider can change rein diagonally across the ring (MXK or HXF), or straight across the middle (F to B), or through a circle.

Collection. Collection shortens the horse's frame between the rider's legs and hands so that his hocks are well engaged, his forehand is elevated, and his neck is raised and arched. The tempo of the gait remains the same but the horse covers less ground; he lifts his legs higher and takes shorter, lighter, more cadenced steps. Collection is characterized by energy, the feeling that the horse's lowered hindquarters are a coiled spring ready to expand. (Also see *extension.*)

Engagement. The horse moves his hind legs farther under his body so that he can balance himself and support additional weight through his hindquarters. At the halt, a green horse will begin to walk with his front leg, but when a horse is engaged he will move his hind leg first.

Extension. Extension lengthens the horse's frame so that the horse goes forward with increased impulsion and a lowered head and neck, his stride lengthened to the utmost. The tempo of the gait remains the same but the horse covers more ground. (Also see *collection.*)

Flexion. The horse responds to the influence of the rider's legs and hands by bending his joints; specifically, by yielding at the poll and relaxing his jaw.

Forehand. The horse's front legs, head, neck, shoulders, and withers.

Forward. The horse is always reaching for a contact with the rider's hands, even at the halt. In order to do this, he must be moving straight, with his hind legs engaged under his body. The horse must be eager, unafraid, and relaxed.

Free walk. The horse is encouraged to stretch his head and neck down and to relax while still overstepping the tracks of his forehand with his hind feet. In all but international level tests the rider is asked to leave the arena at a free walk on a loose rein. (Also see *loose rein.*)

Gaits. The horse has three natural gaits—the walk, trot, and canter. Some people use the word "pace" interchangeably. All three gaits are required at all levels of dressage competition in varying degrees of collection and extension, e.g., working trot, collected trot, medium trot, and extended trot.

Half-halt. A fractional pause in the horse's forward movement during which the rider asks the horse for additional impulsion; for instance, in order to prepare the horse for a transition to another gait.

Halt. Refers to the act of stopping the horse and also to the horse's position once he has stopped moving: he is straight and remains motionless with his weight balanced evenly over all four legs.

Hindquarters. The horse's hind legs, rump, and croup.

Impulsion. A thrusting action originating from the hindquarters that is a result of the horse engaging his hind legs under his body. The horse reaches forward with his hind legs rather than pushes from behind. Impulsion gives energy, brilliance, and keenness to the horse's movements.

Inside. The side away from the rail, or on the inside of any curve or circle. The rider's inside leg is the leg on the "inward" side of the ring. In lateral movements, *inside* refers to the side toward which the horse is bent.

Lateral bend. The horse's spine is bending to the curve of a circle.

Leg-yield. A lateral movement used to teach obediance in addition to suppling. The horse learns to move forward and sideways away from the leg aid.

Long rein. The reins are stretched to the utmost, but the rider maintains very light contact with the horse's mouth. In international level tests the rider is asked to leave the arena at a free walk on a long rein.

Loose rein. The reins are slack; the rider has no contact with the horse's mouth. By letting the reins slip loosely through his fingers, the rider allows the horse to relax by stretching his head and neck as far down as he pleases. (Also see *free walk.*)

On the bit. The horse maintains a light, elastic contact with the rider's hands through the reins. Since the reins themselves have no "give," the contact is a result of the horse yielding at the poll and jaw and the rider "receiving" with flexible hands. A horse is said to be on the bit when he moves forward with balance and impulsion in response to the rider's aids with his neck raised or lowered (depending on the degree of collection or extension), without resisting or depending on the rider's hands for support, so that rein contact between rider and horse remains supple and light.

Outside. The side closest to the rail, or to the outside of any curve or circle. The rider's outside leg is the leg that's next to the rail. In lateral movements, *outside* refers to the side opposite to which the horse is bent.

Resistance. The horse lets the rider know he would rather not do what the rider is asking of him by grinding his teeth, wringing his tail, hollowing his back, sticking his nose in the air or tucking it into his chest, pulling on the rider's hands, getting his tongue over the bit, etc.

Rhythm. The internal beat of the gait, which the rider can determine by listening to the horse's hoofbeats. The walk has a four-beat rhythm, the trot has a two-beat rhythm, and the canter has a three-beat rhythm. The rhythm must remain steady and consistent, with an equal interval of time between each beat. A good way to achieve rhythmic gaits is to ride to music or a metronome. (Also see *tempo.*)

Seat. The rider's physical position in the saddle. A dressage rider needs a balanced seat: he should be sitting straight in the deepest part of the saddle, erect but relaxed, allowing himself to follow the movements of the horse and able to use his aids without changing the position of the rest of his body.

Serpentine. A series of loops or half-circles all the same size, used to teach the horse lateral bending. Serpentines help to develop and supple both sides of the horse equally.

Straight. One of the fundamental rules of dressage is "straighten your horse and ride him forward." A horse is straight when his backbone is parallel to the track he's on and his hind feet follow the track of his forefeet without deviating to the side.

Suspension. That moment in the trot or canter when the horse has all four feet off the ground.

Tempo. Frequency of footfalls. The tempo of a given gait doesn't speed or slow down or change in any way from collection to extension; the number of times the horse's feet hit the ground per minute remains exactly the same. The words "rhythm" and "tempo" are often used interchangeably. (Also see *rhythm*.)

Track. Track has several meanings. One refers to the course the rider takes around the ring: "Tracking to the right" means the rider is going to the right, clockwise, or on the right rein. It also refers to the course the horse is on, and to the horse's actual hoofprints: a horse should bend according to the track (course) of a circle so that his hind feet step into the tracks (hoofprints) of his forehand.

Transition. Any change of gait or movement or lengthening of stride. Transitions must be smooth and quickly and quietly done, but not hurried.

Trot. One of the horse's natural gaits. The legs move diagonally (left hind and right fore together, then right hind and left fore together) in a two-beat rhythm, with a moment of suspension between each beat. A horse should be able to complete approximately 35 strides per minute at the working trot.

Walk. One of the horse's natural gaits. The sequence of legs is right hind, right fore, left hind, and left fore. The walk has a four-beat rhythm with no moment of suspension. A horse should be able to complete approximately 25 strides per minute at the working walk.

Index